The Mystery of Faith

A Study of the Structural Elements of the Order of the Mass

by Lawrence J. Johnson

Federation of Diocesan Liturgical Commissions
415 Michigan Avenue, N.E.
Suite 70
Washington, D.C. 20017
Phone: 202-635-6990
FAX: 202-529-2452

Acknowledgements

Excerpts from the *General Instruction of the Roman Missal (Third Typical Edition)* © 2002 International Commission on English in the Liturgy, Inc. (ICEL); excerpts from the Introduction to the *Lectionary for Mass* © 1981, 1998 (altered by the National Conference of Catholic Bishops), ICEL; excerpts from the English translation of *Dedication of a Church and an Altar* © 1978, ICEL; excerpts from *Documents on the Liturgy, 1963-1979: Conciliar, Papal and Curial Texts* © 1982, ICEL. All rights reserved.

Excerpts from the *Norms for the Distribution and Reception of Holy Communion under both Kinds in the Dioceses of the United States* © 2002; *Third Instruction on the Correct Implementation of the Constitution on the Sacred Liturgy* © 1970; *Music in Catholic Worship, Revised Edition* © 1983; *The Body of Christ* © 1977; *The Sign of Peace* © 1977; *Liturgical Music Today* © 1982, United States Conference of Catholic Bishops, Inc. Washington DC. All rights reserved. No part of this work may be reproduced or transmitted in any form of by any means, electronic or mechanical, including photocopying, recording, or by any information storage and retrieval system, without permission in writing from the copyright holder.

Excerpts from the documents of the Second Vatican Council: *Constitution on the Sacred Liturgy* and the *Constitution on Divine Revelation* taken from the *Documents of Vatican II*, edited by Walter M. Abbott, S.J., © 1966, The America Press.

Artwork by Rev. Francis George.

The Mystery of Faith: A Study of the Structural Elements of the Order of the Mass prepared by the Federation of Diocesan Liturgical Commissions (FDLC) in cooperation with the Bishops' Committee on the Liturgy who initiated this study. © 1981, revised edition 2003. Reprinted with corrections 2004, 2005, 2006. All rights reserved.

The Federation of Diocesan Liturgical Commissions (FDLC) 415 Michigan Avenue, NE, Suite 70, Washington, D.C. 20017. Web: fdlc.org; email: publications@fdlc.org; fax: 202-529-2452; voice: 202-635-6990.

Table of Contents

Introduction to the 2003 Edition i
Introduction to the First Edition (1981) ii

Introductory Rites
    General Overview 1
    Entrance Procession 3
    Entrance Song 5
    Veneration of the Altar 7
    Sign of the Cross; Greeting; Introduction 10
    The Act of Penitence 13
    Sunday Renewal of Baptism 15
    "Lord Have Mercy" 16
    "Glory to God" 18
    The Collect 20

Liturgy of the Word
    General Overview 25
    First Reading 32
    Responsorial Psalm 34
    Second Reading 37
    Alleluia/Gospel Acclamation; Sequence 38
    Gospel 41
    Homily 44
    Profession of Faith 47
    Prayer of the Faithful 50

Liturgy of the Eucharist
    General Overview 55

A. Preparation of the Gifts
    General Overview 57
    Preparation of the Altar 59
    Presentation of the Gifts 61
    Music at the Presentation/ Preparation of the Gifts 63
    Prayers at the Preparation of the Gifts 65
    Mixing of Water and Wine 67
    "Lord God, We Ask You" 68
    Incensation 69
    Washing of Hands 71
    Prayer over the Offerings and Its Invitation 72

B. Eucharistic Prayer
    General Overview 74
    Preface 79
    "Holy, Holy, Holy Lord" 81
    Epiclesis 83
    Narrative of the Institution 85
    Memorial Acclamation 87
    Anamnesis 89
    Offering 91

  Intercessions 93
  Final Doxology 95
 C. Communion Rite
  General Overview 97
  Lord's Prayer 99
  Rite of Peace 101
  Breaking of Bread 103
  Commingling 105
  "Lamb of God" 106
  Private Preparation of Priest and People 108
  Invitation to Communion 109
  Distribution of the Eucharist 110
  Music at Communion 117
  Purification of the Vessels 119
  Silent Prayer/Song Of Praise 122
  Prayer after Communion 124
Concluding Rites 127
 General Overview 129
 Announcements 131
 Greeting and Blessing 132
 Dismissal 134
 Veneration of the Altar 136
 Recessional 137
Selected Bibliography 138

Introduction to the 2003 Edition

In 1981, with the encouragement of the NCCB Committee on the Liturgy, the Federation of Diocesan Liturgical Commissions undertook the development of a pastoral commentary on the Order of Mass designed to place the rites of the Sacred Liturgy within the context of the Church's rich liturgical tradition. Since its publication, *The Mystery of Faith* has helped almost one hundred thousand of the faithful to deepen their appreciation of the Liturgy they are called to celebrate each week.

Now, in the first years of a new millennium, we have been given a third edition of the *Roman Missal* and a major Encyclical on the Eucharist, *Ecclesia de Eucharistia*. The Federation has, therefore, completely revised *The Mystery of Faith* in the light of the *Missale Romanum, editio typica tertia*, so that yet another generation may derive from the celebration of Mass, "those fruits for the sake of which Christ the Lord instituted the Eucharistic Sacrifice of his Body and Blood and entrusted it to the Church, his beloved Bride, as the memorial of his Passion and Resurrection" (*General Instruction of the Roman Missal*, no. 17).

As Bishops, their diocesan offices for worship, pastors and pastoral liturgists throughout the country continue their careful implementation of this latest stage of the liturgical renewal, the present work can help to shed light on the meaning of the Church's current liturgical rites and practices. Taken together with the *General Instruction of the Roman Missal* and the BCL's *Introduction to the Order of Mass*, this newly-revised edition of *The Mystery of Faith* can serve as part of a comprehensive program whereby each worshipper's sense of the right and responsibility to participate in the Sacred Mysteries is deepened.

The Liturgical reform of the Second Vatican Council has, in the words of Pope John Paul II, "greatly contributed to a more conscious, active and fruitful participation in the Holy Sacrifice of the altar on the part of the faithful" (*Ecclesia de Eucharistia*, no. 10). It is my hope that this revised edition of *The Mystery of Faith* will continue to lead us all to a deeper appreciation of the source and summit of our life in Christ, the very heart of the mystery of the Church (See *Ecclesia de Eucharistia*, no. 1).

Cardinal Francis George, O.M.I.
Archbishop of Chicago
Chairman
USCCB Committee on the Liturgy

Introduction to the First Edition (1981)

One of the fundamental principles for the revision of the liturgy after Vatican Council II was that the liturgy is the prayer of the entire Church. Operating from this sound theological premise, it follows that the prayer of the Church, if it is to be truly that, must be of such a nature that all of the faithful are able to participate in it with understanding. Thus, the Fathers of the Council recognized the basic need for the reintroduction of the vernacular in the liturgy. They also clearly foresaw the need to revise the existing liturgical rites in such a manner that the nature and purpose of their various elements, as well as their relationship, might be clearly understood by all who gather to pray. All of this was undertaken in order that the "devout and active participation by the faithful may be more clearly accomplished" (Constitution on the Liturgy, no. 53).

Most Catholics are familiar with the fruits of the Council's liturgical challenges. This is true especially with the familiarity they have with the revised Order of Mass, the liturgy celebrated by the entire Church with the greatest frequency. It is central to the life and mission of the Church.

Like all liturgical prayer, the eucharist needs to be celebrated with great faith. It is, in fact, the Mystery of Faith, the memorial of the death and resurrection of the Lord Jesus. Yet, one's faithful stance in the presence of the great Mystery of Faith does not eliminate the need for personal understanding of what is transpiring as the Church proclaims its great prayer of praise and thanksgiving. Those gathered to celebrate Mass, clergy and laity alike, are called upon to do so with intelligent participation.

The ritual elements of the Order of Mass speak clearly and eloquently, needing little explanation. Yet, some should be studied in the light of the historical practice of the Church, the post-conciliar liturgical documents, and the experience that comes from the use of the revised *Ordo* for more than a decade in the USA. Most Catholics, even those who participate in the eucharist frequently, have never taken time out to study, in a systematic manner, the structural elements of the Mass. …

In a sense, then, this book is a response to a recent Vatican Instruction: "Most of the difficulties encountered in putting into practice the reform of the liturgy and especially the reform of the Mass stem from the fact that neither priests nor faithful have perhaps been sufficiently aware of the theological and spiritual reasons for which the changes have been made, in accordance with the principles laid down by the Council" (*Inaestimabile Donum*).

This is a workbook. It was designed by the Bishops' Committee on the Liturgy, in cooperation with the Federation of Diocesan Liturgical Commissions, in order to offer all Catholics the opportunity to study the elements of the Order of Mass in a systematic manner. Not only can it be used fruitfully by interested individuals, but it is especially prepared for group use. It is recommended to parish liturgy committees as their working study-agenda for a complete year of meetings. The workbook could also be introduced into the curriculum of adult education courses, religious education classes, etc.

One of the positive features of the workbook is its clearly defined focus: it is a study of the structural elements of the Order of Mass. In this light, however, a word of caution is still necessary. As you use the book you might want to broaden its scope; you might even criticize the book for not touching other areas. But remember: it was designed for one purpose—the study of structural elements. Note especially that this is not a workbook for the study of liturgical texts or their English translation, as used in the Order of Mass, and included in the lectionary or sacramentary. Nor is this a study of the function and roles of the liturgical ministers within the celebration of the eucharist. All of these are necessary and are useful areas of study, but are beyond the scope of this present work.

One final word would be in place concerning the title of this workbook. *Mysterium Fidei* (The Mystery of Faith) is the title of Pope Paul VI's encyclical on the eucharist published on September 3, 1965. Recall the opening words of Pope Paul's encyclical letter: "The Mystery of Faith, that is the ineffable gift of the eucharist which she has received from Christ her spouse as a pledge of his boundless love, the Catholic Church has ever guarded devoutly as a most precious treasure." It is the same Mystery of Faith that the Church continues to celebrate: It is the same Mystery of Faith that it proclaims. It is the same Mystery of Faith that continually transforms it into what it is not yet.

Reverend Thomas A. Krosnicki, SVD
Executive Director, Bishops' Committee on the Liturgy

Reverend Carl A. Last
Executive Secretary, FDLC

Introductory Rites

1
General Overview

Historical Survey

As early as the mid-second century the celebration of the Eucharist, already separated from its setting within a regular meal, was usually preceded by a Scripture service. The people gathered in silence and, when all had arrived, a lector began to proclaim the word. This ancient practice of beginning immediately with the readings was preserved in the Roman Liturgy of Good Friday till 1956.

But the psychological desire to give a definitive starting point to the celebration and to provide an initial experience of prayer resulted in the gradual development of various introductory rites and formulas. In fifth-century Africa St. Augustine greeted the people before the Scriptures were proclaimed. In late seventh-century Rome the Pope with his ministers passed through the assembly in procession and then began with an initial prayer. During centuries to come other elements, often of a private nature and reflecting the piety of generations and cultures, were added before the Scripture proclamations.

Although not greatly reducing the number of introductory rites, the Order of Mass has at least given them a public character; it has also attempted to arrange them in a structure that is more logical and adaptable.

Documentation

General Instruction of the Roman Missal, Third Typical Edition

46. The rites preceding the Liturgy of the Word, namely the entrance, greeting, act of penitence, *Kyrie*, *Gloria*, and collect, have the character of a beginning, introduction, and preparation.
    Their purpose is to ensure that the faithful who come together as one establish communion and dispose themselves to listen properly to God's word and to celebrate the Eucharist worthily.
    In certain celebrations that are combined with Mass according to the norms of the liturgical books, the Introductory Rites are omitted or performed in a particular way.

42. … a common posture, to be observed by all participants, is a sign of the unity of the members of the Christian community gathered for the Sacred Liturgy: it both expresses and fosters the intention and spiritual attitude of the participants.

43. The faithful should stand from the beginning of the entrance chant, or while the priest approaches the altar, until the end of the collect …
    With a view to a uniformity in gestures and postures during one and the same celebration, the faithful should follow the directions which the deacon, lay minister, or priest gives according to whatever is indicated in the Missal.

Reflection

These rites, serving to introduce and prepare for the Liturgy of the Word and the Liturgy of the Eucharist, are to help the people become a community at worship, an assembly convoked by God. The people, gathering in response to God's call, come together in a spirit of friendliness and hospitality. By celebrating these rites they deepen their unity as a people among whom the Lord is present.

Structurally, these rites are of secondary importance and are celebrated as such. Their major elements are the celebrant's greeting and the people's response (or perhaps the entrance song) and the Opening Prayer or Collect.

Suggested Questions for Discussion

1. How are the people greeted as they gather? By whom are they greeted?
2. How are the people prepared and encouraged to celebrate the liturgy?
3. What is the purpose of the Introductory Rites?
4. What are their major elements?
5. At what times during the introductory rites does the celebrant need the Missal?

2
Entrance Procession

Historical Survey

Once the Church began to celebrate the Eucharist within large buildings, it was natural to utilize the space these structures provided. Most probably some type of formal entrance into the basilica already existed by the fourth century. An expansion of this action eventually occurred. Since the sacristy was located close to the entrance of the major churches at Rome, the Pope accompanied by a large retinue of ministers entered the church from the sacristy and solemnly processed from the church's door to the altar. The precise period when this solemn entrance developed is not known; it is attested for the papal Mass shortly after 701 A.D. Just before the various ministers entered the church, an acolyte solemnly carried in the book containing the gospel passages. Outside Rome, where there were fewer ministers, the procession was more modest. But as the Mass was gradually linked to the Liturgy of the Hours for which the clergy were already assembled, sacristies came to be located in proximity to the sanctuary. Consequently, the procession was generally abbreviated or fell into complete disuse. Today it has been restored, usually with the priest and ministers processing from the rear of the church.

Documentation

General Instruction of the Roman Missal, Third Typical Edition

120. Once the people have gathered, the priest and ministers, clad in the sacred vestments, go in procession to the altar in this order:
    a) the thurifer carrying a thurible with burning incense, if incense is used;
    b) the ministers who carry lighted candles, and between them an acolyte or other minister with the cross;
    c) the acolytes and the other ministers;
    d) A lector, who may carry the Book of the Gospels (though not the Lectionary), which should be slightly elevated;
    e) the priest who is to celebrate the Mass.
    If incense is used, before the procession begins, the priest puts some in the censer (thurible) and blesses it with the sign of the cross while saying nothing.

Reflection

The entrance procession is not just a functional action of solemnly introducing the priest and other ministers to the sanctuary; it is also a visual expression of the people becoming a liturgical community, of being together as a people, a people who have gathered in response to God's invitation. This liturgical assembly visibly manifests at a determined time and in a specified place the presence of Christ and the very nature of the Church whose members possess distinct offices and ministries.

Thus the procession, together with its accompanying song, is a sign of the self-identity of both ministers and people.

Suggested Questions for Discussion

1. What is the purpose of the Entrance procession?
2. Is it always desirable to have an Entrance procession?
3. Are there particular seasons or occasions when a more solemn procession is appropriate?
4. Does the procession always have to include all the ministers of the celebration?
5. Should those who are not ministers ever be included in the procession?
6. Is there ever a danger of symbolically overloading the procession?
7. What is the route of the procession? How long does it take? What is its pace?
8. What attention is given to the position and spacing of the procession's participants?
9. In what manner is the Book of the Gospels carried?
10. Is the Book of the Gospels to be used only at Sunday celebrations?
11. How is the assembly notified as to when to stand?
12. On what occasions would incense be appropriately used during the celebration?
13. May the procession ever be omitted?

3
Entrance Song

Historical Survey

The majority of the western rites have traditionally accompanied the entrance procession with song. At Rome the members of the *schola cantorum* (a trained body of singers) arranged themselves in two double rows at the entrance to the sanctuary. In antiphonal fashion these two choruses sang the Entrance song or Introit, i.e., a psalm which began and concluded with a short antiphon whose text was taken from the psalm itself, the epistle of the day, or even from a non biblical source. During Carolingian times (eighth and ninth centuries) an attempt was made to have the whole assembly sing the concluding "Glory be to the Father." Eventually two major factors contributed to a curtailment of the number of verses sung: the rapid elaboration of melody and the abbreviation of the procession itself. As a result, the singing was reduced to the antiphon, one psalm verse, the doxology, and the repetition of the antiphon. The Introit became an independent chant frequently begun when the priest reached the altar. If not sung, it was recited by the priest after the prayers at the foot of the altar. The Entrance song, in which the whole assembly normally participates, once again accompanies the procession of the priest and other ministers. Great freedom is allowed in regard to the choice of its text.

Documentation

General Instruction of the Roman Missal, Third Typical Edition

47. After the people have gathered, the Entrance chant begins as the priest enters with the deacon and ministers. The purpose of this chant is to open the celebration, foster the unity of those who have been gathered, introduce their thoughts to the mystery of the liturgical season or festivity, and accompany the procession of the priest and ministers.

48. The singing at this time is done either alternately by the choir and the people or in a similar way by the cantor and the people, or entirely by the people, or by the choir alone. In the dioceses of the United States of America there are four options for the Entrance Chant: (1) the antiphon from the Roman Missal or the Psalm from the Roman Gradual as set to music there or in another musical setting; (2) the seasonal antiphon and Psalm of the Simple Gradual; (3) a song from another collection of psalms and antiphons, approved by the Conference of Bishops or the Diocesan Bishop, including psalms arranged in responsorial or metrical forms; (4) a suitable liturgical song similarly approved by the Conference of Bishops or the Diocesan Bishop.
    If there is no singing at the entrance, the antiphon in the Missal is recited either by the faithful, or by some of them, or by a lector; otherwise, it is recited by the priest himself, who may even adapt it as an introductory explanation (cf. … no. 31).

121. During the procession to the altar, the Entrance chant takes place …

Music in Catholic Worship

61. The entrance song should create an atmosphere of celebration. It helps put the assembly in the proper frame of mind for listening to the Word of God. It helps people to become

conscious of themselves as a worshipping community. The choice of texts for the entrance song should not conflict with these purposes. In general, during the most important seasons of the Church year—Easter, Lent, Christmas, and Advent—it is preferable that most songs used at the entrance be seasonal in nature (NCCB, November 1969).

Liturgical Music Today

18. Processional chants accompany an action. In some cases they have another function. The entrance song serves to gather and unite the assembly and set the tone for the celebration as much as to conduct the ministers into the sanctuary …

19. While the responsorial form of singing is especially suitable for processions, the metrical hymn can also fulfill the function of the entrance song. If, however, a metrical hymn with several verses is selected, its form should be respected. The progression of text and music must be allowed to play out its course and achieve its purpose musically and poetically. In other words, the hymn should not be ended indiscriminately at the end of the procession.

Reflection

The purpose of the Entrance song is "to open the celebration, foster the unity of those who have been gathered, introduce their thoughts to the mystery of the liturgical season or festivity, and accompany the procession of the priest and ministers." (GIRM no. 47). This song, designed to accompany a procession, is the first strictly liturgical action of a people among whom Christ is active and present. Uniting the members of the community, the song may assume the form of Psalmody, which is traditional in the Roman Mass, or of hymnody.

Suggested Questions for Discussion

1. In what way can this piece of music be called an "Entrance" song?
2. What is the purpose of the Entrance song?
3. Does it serve as a "greeting" of the presiding minister?
4. Is it more to accompany the procession or to serve as an opening for the celebration?
5. What are the principles governing the choice of its text and music?
6. What style of music reflects the character of an accompaniment to a procession? Of a gathering song?
7. Is psalmody appropriate? Is it ever used?
8. What about a litany?
9. Would it ever be desirable not to have an Entrance song?
10. May instrumental music or silence ever substitute for the Entrance song?
11. When there is no Entrance song, why is the antiphon given in the Missal to be recited?
12. How important is it that the presiding celebrant and other ministers join in the singing?

4
Veneration of the Altar

Historical Survey

In ancient times the kiss as a sign of greeting was used to show reverence for temples and images of the gods. It seems that the table was likewise honored before the family meal in places where every meal was considered sacred, where the participants in the meal were seen as either hosts or guests of the household gods. By the fourth century Christian worship appropriated this sign of honor since the altar was the "table of the Lord." As the altar came to be constructed of stone, it was looked upon as the symbol of Christ, the cornerstone and spiritual rock of the Church. With the growth of the cult of the martyrs, relics were placed beneath the altar, and the kiss was seen as greeting the saints and through them the whole Church triumphant. Until the thirteenth century the altar was kissed only three times during Mass: at the beginning, during the Eucharistic Prayer, and before the dismissal. A century later this sign so multiplied that the importance of the original kiss at the beginning and end of the celebration was perhaps obscured. Today the altar is venerated with a kiss only at the beginning and end of Mass.

The use of incense at worship is of great antiquity. In pre–Christian times it had numerous meanings: a symbol of sacrifice, a festive accompaniment for processions, a sign of honor, a means of purification and of expelling evil spirits. Christians first rejected the use of incense since it was closely associated with pagan cult. But after the time of Constantine (280–337) various dignities accorded to major Roman officials were transferred to the Bishop of Rome and the other Bishops. Thus it became customary to bear incense before them as they entered the church in procession—a vestige of the Roman-Byzantine ceremonial of carrying incense before the Emperor. A formal incensation of the altar in the Roman Mass, however, is only attested in the eleventh century. Scholars suggest that the original meaning of the practice was purification and protection. Furthermore, there was also the Old Testament injunction that the service of the High Priest was to begin with incense (see Leviticus 16:12). At any rate, this incensation was generally interpreted as a sign of the altar's being encircled by an atmosphere of prayer and sacrifice ascending to God.

Documentation

General Instruction of the Roman Missal, Third Typical Edition

49. When they reach the sanctuary, the priest, the deacon, and the ministers reverence the altar with a profound bow.
    As an expression of veneration, moreover, the priest and deacon then kiss the altar itself; as the occasion suggests, the priest also incenses the cross and the altar.

122. On reaching the altar, the priest and ministers make a profound bow.
    The cross adorned with a figure of Christ crucified and perhaps carried in procession may be placed next to the altar to serve as the altar cross, in which case it

ought to be the only cross used; otherwise it is put away in a dignified place. In addition, the candlesticks are placed on the altar or near it. It is a praiseworthy practice that the Book of the Gospels be placed upon the altar.

123. The priest goes up to the altar and venerates it with a kiss. Then, as the occasion suggests, he incenses the cross and the altar, walking around the latter.

276. Thurification or incensation is an expression of reverence and of prayer, as is signified in Sacred Scripture (cf. Ps 141 [140]:2, Rev 8:3).

    Incense may be used if desired in any form of Mass:
    a) during the Entrance procession;
    b) at the beginning of Mass, to incense the cross and the altar ; ...

277. The priest, having put incense into the thurible, blesses it with the sign of the Cross, without saying anything.

    Before and after an incensation, a profound bow is made to the person or object that is incensed, except for the incensation of the altar and the offerings for the Sacrifice of the Mass.

    The following are incensed with three swings of the thurible: the Most Blessed Sacrament, a relic of the Holy Cross and images of the Lord exposed for public veneration, the offerings for the sacrifice of the Mass, the altar cross, the Book of the Gospels, the Paschal Candle, the priest, and the people. ...

    The altar is incensed with a series of single swings of the thurible in this way:
    a) If the altar is freestanding with respect to the wall, the priest incenses walking around it;
    b) If the altar is not freestanding, the priest incenses it while walking first to the righthand side, then to the left.

    The cross, if situated on or near the altar, is incensed by the priest before he incenses the altar; otherwise, he incenses it when he passes in front of it.

Reflection

The altar "is by its very nature a table of sacrifice and at the same time a table of the paschal banquet" *(Dedication of a Church and an Altar,* Chapter IV, no. 4). It is the symbol of Christ as well as of the whole Christian community since "Christians who give themselves to prayer, who offer petitions to God and present sacrifices of supplication, are the living stones from which the Lord Jesus builds the Church's altar" (ibid., no. 2). The veneration of the altar at the beginning of the celebration is an act of greeting which recalls that the common table is holy and sacred to the action of the assembly. It is the place from which prayer ascends like incense before God (see Psalm 141:2). It is venerated by the presiding priest in the name of all.

Suggested Questions for Discussion

1. What is the purpose of kissing and incensing the altar?
2. Are there other ways of venerating the altar?
3. Is the altar treated with reverence both within and outside the liturgical celebration?
4. How would you characterize the usual manner of kissing the altar: hurried? embarrassed? loving? deliberate?

5. What makes the use of incense at the beginning of the celebration an appropriate sign for a given occasion?
6. Does this incensation duplicate any other incensations in the Mass?
7. Is the cross to be incensed?
8. Where is the processional cross placed after the procession?
9. Is there a danger of using the altar as a resting place for cruets, towels, pieces of paper, etc.?

5
Sign of the Cross; Greeting; Introduction

Historical Survey

Signing with the cross was a gesture practiced by Christians as early as the second century. By the late fourth century this action was incorporated at many points within the celebration of the sacraments. And yet a signing at the beginning of Mass appeared in the Roman Liturgy only with the medieval introduction of the prayers at the foot of the altar, i.e., private prayers originally said by the priest on the way to the sanctuary.

A greeting extended by the presiding minister, on the other hand, is among the most ancient elements of the introductory rites. At Rome it served as an introduction to the opening prayer of the Mass. The traditional formula in the west (and also in Egypt) has been "The Lord be with you," a text of biblical origins. Although these words appear as a greeting in Ruth 2:4, they are more often found as a simple statement of God's presence in those who are being addressed, e.g., Judges 6:12. The accustomed Latin response *Et cum spiritu tuo* has many parallels in St. Paul, e.g., Galatians 6:18, yet its liturgical meaning appears to be more than a simple expression of good will—the minister is the one whose spirit has received the Spirit of God in Ordination and is thereby a special "servant of Christ" (1 Corinthians 4:1). The Order of Mass provides two additional greetings. The first is the conclusion of St. Paul's Second Letter to the Corinthians (13:13) and is found in some eastern liturgies as introducing the dialogue before the Eucharistic Prayer: *The grace of our Lord Jesus Christ ...* The other is *The grace and peace of God our Father ...*, a formula often used by St. Paul to begin his letters, e.g., Galatians 1:3.

The Order of Mass allows for the presiding priest or some suitable minister to give a short introduction to the celebration. There is no written evidence attesting a similar practice in the early Church.

Documentation

General Instruction of the Roman Missal, Third Typical Edition

50. When the Entrance chant is concluded, the priest stands at the chair and, together with the whole gathering, makes the Sign of the Cross. Then he signifies the presence of the Lord to the community gathered there by means of the Greeting. By this Greeting and the people's response, the mystery of the Church gathered together is made manifest.
    After the greeting of the people, the priest, the deacon, or a lay minister may very briefly introduce the faithful to the Mass of the day.

124. ... once the Entrance chant is concluded, the priest and faithful, all standing, make the Sign of the Cross. The priest says, *In nomine Patris et Filii et Spiritus Sancti (In*

the name of the Father, and of the Son, and of the Holy Spirit). The people answer, *Amen.*

Then, facing the people and extending his hands, the priest greets the people, using one of the formulas indicated. The priest himself or some other minister may also very briefly introduce the faithful to the Mass of the day.

31. It is also up to the priest, in the exercise of his office of presiding over the gathered assemble, to offer certain explanations that are foreseen in the rite itself. … In addition, he may give the faithful a very brief introduction to the Mass of the day (after the initial Greeting and before the Act of Penitence) …

Reflection

The sign of the cross, a traditional prelude to prayer, is a form of self-blessing with strong baptismal overtones: in the rite of Christian initiation a person is signed with the cross, for it is from the victorious Cross of Jesus Christ that salvation comes to us. Moreover, every Christian has been baptized in the name of the Father, Son, and Holy Spirit. The community at worship is first and foremost a baptismal community, and for this reason can gather to celebrate the Lord Jesus.

Romano Guardini (1885–1968), the noted German theologian, wrote: "When we cross ourselves, let it be with a real sign of the cross … let us make a large, unhurried sign, from forehead to breast, from shoulder to shoulder, consciously feeling how it includes the whole of us … It is the holiest of all signs" (*Sacred Signs*, St. Louis, 1956, p. 13ff.).

The Greeting, which is much more than a friendly "Good morning," is both a formalized announcement and wish that the people actually experience the presence and power of the Lord in the community they form. Since Christ is present in the assembly and in its members, the Greeting and the congregation's response express "the mystery of the Church gathered together" (GIRM no. 50).

The introduction, always very brief, should not be a duplication of the Greeting, much less a mini-homily. It may focus upon the special character of the celebration or upon those who are present.

Suggested Questions for Discussion

1. Where does the priest stand after he greets the altar?
2. What is the purpose of the sign of the cross?
3. Does the celebration actually begin with the sign of the cross?
4. How is the sign of the cross made?
5. Might it ever be effective to sing the sign of the cross?
6. What is the purpose of the Greeting?
7. What forms does it take?
8. Does it actually convey the feeling of welcome?
9. Should the greeting be read from the Missal?
10. What type of gesture is used to accompany it?
11. Is it appropriate for the celebrant to extend an informal greeting either before or after the formal Greeting?
12. What is the purpose of the introduction?

13. By whom is it given?
14. Can introductions be misused?
15. What is the role of creativity in these structural elements?
16. Are they ever unduly prolonged?

6
The Act of Penitence

Historical Survey

For centuries the Roman Mass, as generally celebrated, had no penitential rite. The *Confiteor* eventually appeared among the prayers said by the priest and ministers at the foot of the altar and was also said by a minister prior to the distribution of the Eucharist. Yet in both instances these were private rather than public prayers.

Much discussion took place among the artisans of the Order of Mass after the Second Vatican Council. Should a penitential rite be included since the Eucharist itself is a sacrament of reconciliation? And if so, should such a rite be used at all times? What would the most appropriate location for a penitential rite? After much deliberation it was decided to place a simple penitential rite at the beginning of the celebration. In a way this decision reflects both Scripture and tradition. In Matthew 5:23–25 Christ calls for reconciliation with others before offering sacrifice. Moreover, an ancient document known as the *Didache* states that on the Lord's Day people are to come together to break bread and to give thanks "after first confessing their sins" so that the sacrifice will be pure.

The rite has a four-part structure. After an invitation requesting the community to recall its sinfulness, there is a period of silent reflection. A common proclamation that all are sinners before God follows. This may be a shorter and more simplified form of the traditional (*Confiteor*), with its mention of the social dimension of sin, or one of the two sets of invocations addressed to Christ and incorporating the *Kyrie*: the first set consists of two verses, each having a response by the people; the second consists of three invocations (with the assembly's response) addressed to Christ (eight possible models are given in the Missal). The priest concludes with a prayer requesting forgiveness.

Documentation

General Instruction of the Roman Missal, Third Typical Edition

51. Then the priest invites those present to take part in the Act of Penitence, which, after a brief pause for silence, the entire community carries out through a formula of general confession. The rite concludes with the priest's absolution, which, however, lacks the efficacy of the Sacrament of Penance.

45. Sacred silence also, as part of the celebration, is to be observed at the designated times. Its purpose, however, depends on the time it occurs in each part of the celebration. Thus within the Act of Penitence … all recollect themselves …

Liturgical Music Today

21. The litany of the third form of the penitential rite at Mass increasingly is being set to music for deacon (or cantor) and assembly, with the people's response made in Greek or English. This litany functions as a "general confession made by the entire assembly" (GIRM 29 [51]) and as praise of Christ's compassionate love and mercy. It is

appropriately sung at more solemn celebrations and in Advent and Lent when the Gloria is omitted (GIRM 31 [53]).

Reflection

What the Church celebrates in the Liturgy is Christ and our life in Christ; yet nonetheless its members cannot fail to acknowledge sin and guilt. And so in the Act of Penitence the whole assembly, proclaiming itself sinful before a merciful and forgiving God, shows that it is a community ever converting, ever in need of reconciliation with God and others. The people are not called to make an "examination of conscience" but rather to make a proclamation of faith in a God who is loving, kind, and the source of all reconciliation and healing. The focus is not on us but on the merciful God.

Suggested Questions for Discussion

1. What is the purpose of the Act of Penitence?
2. Are there certain seasons when the penitential rite should be more pronounced?
3. In what ways may the invitation of the priest be adapted to the occasion?
4. What gestures or postures are expressive of penance? Of reconciliation?
5. What is the length of the silence that follows the invitation given by the priest?
6. What are the characteristics of the invocations?
7. Does a sign of the cross accompany the prayer requesting forgiveness?

7
Sunday Renewal of Baptism

Historical Survey
Till recently a rite known as the *Asperges* was celebrated before the principal Mass on Sunday. The word comes from Psalm 51:9: "Cleanse me of sin with hyssop, that I may be purified." Verses of the psalm were sung while the priest walked through the church and sprinkled holy water over the people. During Paschal time the *Asperges* was replaced by the *Vidi Aquam*, a text based on Ezekiel 47:1, 8, 9: "I saw water flowing out from beneath the threshold of the temple."

This custom, which gained great popularity in the Middle Ages, seems to have originated in eighth-century monasticism as a sign of sanctification. A procession moved through the cloister, and its rooms were sprinkled. Soon the rite was celebrated before the principal Mass in parish churches where it progressively took on a baptismal character. It served as a reminder of the life-giving waters flowing from the font.

Today at all Sunday Masses, including anticipated Masses on Saturday evening, a rite of sprinkling may replace the usual Act of Penitence. Three different prayers are given for the blessing of the water; the third—highlighting the Paschal Mystery—is designated for use during the Easter season. Nonetheless, the rite may be celebrated during any season of the year.

Documentation
General Instruction of the Roman Missal, Third Typical Edition
51. … on Sundays, especially in the Season of Easter, in place of the customary Act of Penitence, from time to time the blessing and sprinkling of water to recall Baptism may take place.

Reflection
The sprinkling with water is a visual reminder of Baptism (the foundational sacrament of all repentance) and the unique character of Sunday. Through the sacraments of Christian initiation we die, are buried, and rise again with Christ: we thereby share in Christ's victory over sin and death. Although the sprinkling is not a penitential rite, nonetheless, every Sunday is a paschal feast celebrating the memorial of the Lord's Resurrection which is the taproot of all reconciliation.

Suggested Questions for Discussion
1. What is the purpose of the Sunday renewal of baptism?
2. What aspect of Baptism is signified by this rite?
3. Are there any seasons when the rite might be either less or more appropriate?
4. What kind of vessel is used for the water?
5. Where is this vessel placed while the water is blessed?
6. Do the people actually feel water when they are sprinkled?
7. What parts of the rite lend themselves to singing?

8
"Lord Have Mercy"

Historical Survey

The presence of the *Kyrie* or the "Lord have mercy" has a long and complex history. As early as the fourth century this acclamation was used in the east as the people's response to every petition in a litany (the word "litany" coming from the Greek and meaning "prayer"). An intention was announced by the deacon, and the congregation gave this standard response. The pattern continued till the end of the litany. Pope Gelasius (492–496) substituted such an eastern form with its Greek response for an older type of intercessory prayer at the conclusion of the Liturgy of the Word. This new litany with its *Kyrie* was then transferred to the beginning of the Mass. Pope Gregory the Great (590–604), desirous of shortening the Mass, allowed the intentions of the litany to be omitted on certain days with only the response being sung. This abbreviated litany eventually became the rule. The number of three *Kyries*, three *Christes*, and three further *Kyries* was fixed in Frankish countries and provided the basis for a trinitarian interpretation. However, in the New Testament and especially in St. Paul the word *Kyrios* refers to Christ and indicates his divinity.

When not occurring in the Act of Penitence itself, the *Kyrie* and *Christe* now serve as a set of acclamations after it. Addressed to Christ, each acclamation is usually doubled but on occasion may be repeated more often. A short verse (trope), also addressed to Christ and not duplicating the Act of Penitence or the Prayer of the Faithful, may be inserted within the acclamations. The congregation acclaims the Lord's presence and power.

Documentation

General Instruction of the Roman Missal, Third Typical Edition

52. After the Act of Penitence, the *Kyrie* is always begun, unless it has already been included as part of the Act of Penitence. Since it is a chant by which the faithful acclaim the Lord and implore his mercy, it is ordinarily done by all, that is, by the people and with the choir or cantor having a part in it.

Music in Catholic Worship

65. This short litany was traditionally a prayer of praise to the risen Christ. He has been raised and made "Lord," and we beg him to show his loving kindness. The six-fold Kyrie of the new order of Mass may be sung in other ways, for example, as a nine-fold chant (cf. GIRM, 30 [52]). It may also be incorporated in the penitential rite, with invocations addressed to Christ. When sung, the setting should be brief and simple in order not to give undue importance to the introductory rites.

Reflection

The acclamation praises the risen Lord for his goodness and implores his bounty on behalf of all humankind. Its object is universal since the concern of the liturgical assembly extends beyond the needs of its own immediate members.

Suggested Questions for Discussion

1. What is the purpose of the *Kyrie* as an acclamation?
2. How does it differ from the Act of Penitence and from the Prayer of the Faithful?
3. Are tropes ever used? Should they be used?
4. Should the *Kyrie* be sung or recited?
5. By whom should it be sung?
6. Who ordinarily leads the acclamation?

9
"Glory to God"

Historical Survey

The *Gloria* is also known as the "greater doxology." Some call it the "Angelic Hymn" since its first words are those of the angels at Bethlehem. It has come down to us from the treasury of early Christian hymns modeled upon the psalms and canticles of the Bible. First found in Greek and Syrian sources, this song of praise was used as an Easter hymn of dawn and gradually found a place at the conclusion of morning prayer in the east. It entered the west, perhaps by way of Gaul, and by the beginning of the sixth century was already incorporated into the Pope's Christmas Mass at Rome, and then at Sundays Masses and Feasts of martyrs when the Bishop presided. The hymn was used by priests only at the Easter Vigil. By the eleventh century it was sung at all Masses on Sundays and festive occasions.

The *Gloria* is a hymn-anthem containing a series of acclamations. The text today mentions all three persons of the Trinity; this trinitarian characteristic is even more pronounced in some of the hymn's early texts.

Set to simple melodies, the *Gloria* was originally a song of the whole assembly. With the development of elaborate musical settings, it came to be chanted by the choir alone. Today the people normally participate in the singing.

Documentation

General Instruction of the Roman Missal, Third Typical Edition

53. The *Gloria* is a very ancient and venerable hymn in which the Church, gathered together in the Holy Spirit, glorifies and entreats God the Father and the Lamb. The text of this hymn may not be replaced by any other text. The *Gloria* is intoned by the priest or, if appropriate, by a cantor or by the choir; but it is sung either by everyone together, or by the people alternately with the choir, or by the choir alone. If not sung, it is to be recited either by all together or by two parts of the congregation responding one to the other.
    It is sung or said on Sundays outside the Seasons of Advent and Lent, on solemnities and feasts, and at special celebrations of a more solemn character.

Music in Catholic Worship

66. This ancient hymn of praise is now given a new poetic and singable translation. It may be introduced by celebrant, cantor, or choir. The restricted use of the Gloria, i.e., only on Sundays outside Advent and Lent and on solemnities and feasts, (GIRM 31 [53]) emphasizes its special and solemn character. The new text offers many opportunities for alternation of choir and people in poetic parallelisms. The "Glory to God" also provides an opportunity for the choir to sing alone on festive occasions.

Reflection

The *Gloria,* a joyful hymn (and hymns are not recited) whose content is primarily that of praising God, emphasizes the festive and special character of certain Sundays and feasts.

Suggested Questions for Discussion
1. What is the purpose of the *Gloria?*
2. Does its present location serve the flow of the introductory rites?
5. Do the people notice the absence of the *Gloria* during Advent and Lent?
6. Do people enjoy singing it?
7. May it be replaced by other hymns of similar character?
8. What are the advantages and disadvantages of singing the Gloria in responsorial fashion?
9. What is the character of this hymn when it is recited?
10. By whom should it be intoned?

10
The Collect

Historical Survey

The presence of this prayer or oration (from the Latin *orare*, i.e., to pray), which has no exact equivalent in ancient non-Roman liturgies, dates from at least the fifth century. After the Entrance procession the presiding celebrant greeted the people; a concise call or invitation to prayer, i.e., the *Let us pray*, followed; the people then prayed in silence; finally the celebrant summed up and concluded the silent prayer of all, as the people responded with their *Amen*. *Amen* is a Hebrew word used to express what is true, namely, "verily." In Scripture we find it as an expression of assent, e.g., Deuteronomy 27:15ff. and 1 Corinthians 14:16. It even stands for the name of Jesus, as in Revelation 3:14. In Gaul the prayer was known as the *collecta*, a prayer which "gathers together" the intentions of the faithful. The Roman Latin texts have been called "linguistic gems" because of their polished style, clarity, spiritual content, conciseness, etc. The unique character of the Collect was obscured by the elimination of the time for common prayer in silence and by the gradual addition of other orations commemorating various saints or mentioning special petitions.

Generally speaking, the orations of the Roman Mass have the same structure: an address, a petition, and a conclusion. Following the structure of pagan prayer forms used at Rome, the address to the Father is at times extended by recalling a particular feast or mystery or motive for the petition. The petition itself, the core of the prayer, usually remains very general since the oration is to sum up the unspoken prayers of all. Finally, the conclusion underlines the mediation of Christ since the prayer of the assembly ascends to the Father "through Jesus Christ" who is our High Priest and Advocate.

During the prayer the celebrant raises and extends his hands, a gesture recalling the praying figures (*orantes*) found in the catacombs of Rome.

In the liturgical renewal after the Second Vatican Council, an effort has been made to restore certain elements of the earlier unique function of the Collect, which is one of the three "presidential orations" in the Mass, by having it follow a time for silent petition and also by stipulating that it is not to be followed by additional requests or commemorations.

The texts of the Collects found in the Roman Missal today are taken from the former Roman Missal and from ancient liturgical books (even those of non-Roman origin), although in the latter case the texts have often been altered. At times it is only the Collect that expresses the particular character of the celebration.

Documentation

General Instruction of the Roman Missal, Third Typical Edition

54. Next the priest invites the people to pray. All, together with the priest, observe a brief silence so that they may be conscious of the fact that they are in God's

presence and may formulate their petitions mentally. Then the priest says the prayer which is customarily known as the Collect and through which the character of the celebration is expressed. In accordance with the ancient tradition of the Church, the collect prayer is usually addressed to God the Father, through Christ, in the Holy Spirit, and is concluded with a trinitarian, that is to say the longer ending, in the following manner:

- If the prayer is directed to the Father: *Per Dominum nostrum Iesum Christum Filium tuum, qui tecum vivit et regnat in unitate Spiritus Sancti, Deus, per omnia saecula saeculorum*;

- If it is directed to the Father, but the Son is mentioned at the end: *Qui tecum vivit et regnat in unitate Spiritus Sancti, Deus, per omnia saecula saeculorum*;

- If it is directed to the Son: *Qui vivis et regnas cum Deo Patre in unitate Spiritus Sancti, Deus, per omnia saecula saeculorum*.

The people, uniting themselves to this entreaty, make the prayer their own with the acclamation *Amen*.

There is always only one collect used in a Mass.

127. With hands joined, the priest then invites the people to pray, saying: *Let us pray*. All pray silently with the priest for a while. Then the priest, with hands outstretched, says the collect, at the end of which the people make the acclamation. *Amen*.

30. Among the parts assigned to the priest, the foremost is the Eucharistic Prayer, which is the high point of the entire celebration. Next are the orations: that is to say, the collect, the prayer over the offerings, and the prayer after Communion. These prayers are addressed to God in the name of the entire holy people and all present, by the priest who presides over the assembly in the person of Christ. It is with good reason, therefore, that they are called the "presidential prayers."

32. The nature of the "presidential" texts demands that they be spoken in a loud and clear voice and that everyone listen with attention. Thus, while the priest is speaking these texts, there should be no other prayers or singing, and the organ or other musical instruments should be silent.

45. Sacred silence also, as part of the celebration, is to be observed at the designated times. Its purpose, however, depends on the time it occurs in each part of the celebration. Thus … after the invitation to pray, all recollect themselves …

Reflection

Serving more as the conclusion and climax of the Introductory Rites and the prayer that has already occurred (rather than an opening prayer), the collect is a prayer of the gathered community whose members are now aware "that they are in God's presence" (GIRM no. 54). After an invitation which may be expanded to focus upon the specific character of the celebration, the assembly silently expresses its needs and desires which are then "gathered up" by the celebrant and presented to the Father through the Son and in the Holy Spirit. All make this prayer their own by acclaiming *Amen*.

Suggested Questions for Discussion

1. What is the purpose of the Collect?
2. In what sense is this prayer an "opening" prayer?
3. Do people generally consider the prayer as the conclusion of the Introductory Rites?
4. When should the invitation and prayer be sung?
5. What gesture is used by the celebrant as he invites all to pray? What is its meaning?
6. What is to happen in the hearts and souls of people during the time for silence?
7. What length of time is necessary for this to happen?
8. What gesture is used by the celebrant as he sums up the prayers of all? What meaning is this gesture to convey?
9. Is it necessary for the priest to request the assembly to be seated after he concludes the prayer?

Liturgy of the Word

11
General Overview

Historical Survey

Although evidence is meager, there is good reason to believe that a proclamation of God's word sometimes took place in conjunction with the early celebration of the Eucharist. The documents attesting to the fact are few, but of considerable weight. Apostolic writings were read at Christian asemblies (see Colossians 4:16, Philemon 2, Revelation 1:3), and it is likely that at least some of these gatherings were for celebrations of the Eucharist. There is also evidence, e.g., Acts 20: 7–8, to suggest that instruction and explanation took place at the eucharistic meal.

And yet it was only subsequent to the separation of the Eucharist from the meal that a more formal scripture service developed, whose structure may have been somewhat influenced by the morning prayer service held in the synagogue. Although the Liturgy of the Word and Liturgy of the Eucharist were often celebrated independently of each other, their general fusion seems to have occurred in the east by the early sixth century. In some regions of the west, however, isolated examples of the Mass beginning without a word service can be found at a later date.

Each major liturgical tradition or Rite (e.g., that of Eastern Syria, Jerusalem, Alexandria, etc.)developed its own number and selection of readings. Whereas four or even six readings occur in some eastern Rites, the general rule is three readings, usually the Prophets, the Apostles, and the Gospel. Many scholars believe that Rome originally had three readings, an arrangement restored on Sundays and major feasts by the present Lectionary.

The Scriptures were primitively read in a semi-continuous manner: the lector read the whole book from beginning to end although certain verses or chapters were omitted. But with the development of the liturgical year, a system of fixed and related readings was gradually established to highlight particular feasts or seasons and to give thematic unity to the readings.

The Lectionary arranges the Sunday readings in a three-year cycle, the characteristic feature of each year being the Gospel: year A is based on Matthew, year B on Mark, and year C on Luke. St. John's Gospel occurs on the first Sundays of Lent, during the Easter season, and on certain Sundays during year B. For weekdays there is a two-year cycle: the Gospels remain the same each year but the first reading varies.

Each reading is concluded by the people's acclamation *Thanks be to God* or *Praise to you, Lord Jesus Christ* (after the Gospel) a custom which goes far back into the history of the Roman Mass. The meaning of the *Deo gratias* has been traditionally understood not only as a "Thank you" but as a sign that the people have actually heard the reading and are assenting to its summons. The introduction to the Lectionary encourages the singing of the acclamations before and after the Gospel; it appears to do likewise for the acclamations after the other readings. In 1991 the Bishops of the United States voted to change the translation of the introductions to these acclamations: from *This is the word of the Lord* to simply *The word of the Lord*; and from *This is the Gospel of the Lord* to *The Gospel of the Lord*.

Documentation

General Instruction of the Roman Missal, Third Typical Edition

29. When the Sacred Scriptures are read in the Church, God himself speaks to his people, and Christ, present in his own word, proclaims the Gospel.
Therefore, all must listen with reverence to the readings from God's word, for they make up an element of greatest importance in the Liturgy. Although in the readings from Sacred Scripture God's word is addressed to all people of every era and is understandable to them, nevertheless, a fuller understanding and a greater effectiveness of the word is fostered by a living commentary on the word, that is, the homily, as part of the liturgical action.

55. The main part of the Liturgy of the Word is made up of the readings from Sacred Scripture together with the chants occurring between them. The homily, Profession of Faith, and Prayer of the Faithful, however, develop and conclude this part of the Mass. For in the readings, as explained by the homily, God speaks to his people, opening up to them the mystery of redemption and salvation and offering them spiritual nourishment; and Christ himself is present in the midst of the faithful through his word. By their silence and singing the people make God's word their own, and they also affirm their adherence to it by means of the Profession of Faith. Finally, having been nourished by it, they pour out their petitions in the Prayer of the Faithful for the needs of the entire Church and for the salvation of the whole world.

56. The Liturgy of the Word is to be celebrated in such a way as to promote meditation, and so any sort of haste that hinders recollection must clearly be avoided. During the Liturgy of the Word, it is also appropriate to include brief periods of silence, accommodated to the gathered assembly, in which, at the prompting of the Holy Spirit, the word of God may be grasped by the heart and a response through prayer may be prepared. It may be appropriate to observe such periods of silence, for example, before the Liturgy of the Word itself begins, after the first and second reading, and lastly at the conclusion of the homily.

57. In the readings, the table of God's word is prepared for the faithful, and the riches of the Bible are opened to them. Hence, it is preferable to maintain the arrangement of the biblical readings, by which light is shed on the unity of both Testaments and of salvation history. Moreover, it is unlawful to substitute other, non-biblical texts for the readings and responsorial Psalm, which contain the word of God.

58. In the celebration of the Mass with a congregation, the readings are always proclaimed from the ambo.

59. By tradition, the function of proclaiming the readings is ministerial, not presidential. The readings, therefore, should be proclaimed by a lector, and the Gospel by a deacon or, in his absence, a priest other than the celebrant. If, however, a deacon or another priest is not present, the priest celebrant himself should read the Gospel. Further, if another suitable lector is also not present, then the priest celebrant should also proclaim the other readings.

    After each reading, whoever reads gives the acclamation, to which the gathered people reply, honoring the word of God that they have received in faith and with grateful hearts.

357. For Sundays and solemnities, three readings are assigned: that is, from a Prophet, an Apostle, and a Gospel. By these the Christian people are brought to know the continuity of the work of salvation according to the God's wonderful plan. These readings should be followed strictly.

    During the Easter Season, according to the tradition of the Church, instead of the reading from the Old Testament, the reading is taken from the Acts of the Apostles.

    For Feasts, on the other hand, two readings are assigned. If, however, according to the norms a feast is raised to the rank of a solemnity, a third reading is added, taken from the Common.

    For memorials of Saints, unless strictly proper readings are given, the readings assigned for the weekday are customarily used. In certain cases, readings are provided that highlight some particular aspect of the spiritual life or activity of the Saint. The use of such readings is not to be insisted upon, unless a pastoral reason suggests it.

358. In the Lectionary for weekdays, readings are provided for each day of every week throughout the entire year; as a result, these readings are for the most part to be used on the days to which they are assigned, unless there occurs a solemnity, feast, or memorial that has its own proper New Testament readings, that is to say, readings in which mention is made of the Saint being celebrated.

    If, however, the continuous reading during the week is interrupted by the occurrence of some solemnity or feast, or some particular celebration, then the priest, taking into consideration the entire week's scheme of readings, is allowed either to combine parts omitted with other readings or to decide which readings are to be preferred over others.

    In Masses with special groups, the priest is allowed to choose texts more suited to the particular celebration, provided they are taken from the texts of an approved lectionary.

359. In addition, the Lectionary has a special selection of texts from Sacred Scripture for Ritual Masses into which certain Sacraments or Sacramentals are incorporated, or for Masses that are celebrated for certain needs.

Selections of readings of this kind have been established in this way, so that through a more apt hearing of the word of God the faithful may be led to a fuller understanding of the mystery in which they are participating and may be brought to a more ardent love of the word of God.

As a result, texts spoken in the celebration are to be chosen keeping in mind both a suitable pastoral reason and the options allowed in this matter.

31. It is also up to the priest, in the exercise of his office of presiding over the gathered assembly, to offer certain explanations that are foreseen in the rite itself ... In addition, he may give the faithful a very brief introduction ... to the Liturgy of the Word (before the readings) ...

43. The faithful should stand ... for the Alleluia chant before the Gospel; while the Gospel itself is proclaimed; during the Profession of Faith and the Prayer of the Faithful ...

    They should, however, sit while the readings before the Gospel and the responsorial Psalm are proclaimed and for the homily ...

    With a view to a uniformity in gestures and postures during one and the same celebration, the faithful should follow the directions which the deacon, lay minister, or priest gives according to whatever is indicated in the Missal.

135. If no lector is present, the priest himself proclaims all the readings and the Psalm, standing at the ambo. ...

Lectionary for Mass: Introduction

12. In the celebration of Mass the biblical readings with their accompanying chants from the Sacred Scriptures may not be omitted, shortened, or, worse still, replaced by nonbiblical readings. For it is out of the word of God handed down in writing that even now "God speaks to his people" and it is from the continued use of Sacred Scripture that the people of God, docile to the Holy Spirit under the light of faith, is enabled to bear witness to Christ before the world by its manner of life.

13. The reading of the Gospel is the high point of the Liturgy of the Word. For this the other readings, in their established sequence from the Old to the New Testament, prepare the assembly.

14. A speaking style on the part of the readers that is audible, clear, and intelligent is the first means of transmitting the word of God properly to the congregation. The readings, taken from the approved editions, may be sung in a way suited to different languages. This singing, however, must serve to bring out the sense of the words, not obscure them. On occasions when the readings are in Latin, the manner given in the *Ordo cantus Missae* is to be maintained.

15. There may be concise introductions before the readings, especially the first. The style proper to such comments must be respected, that is, they must be simple, faithful to the text, brief, well prepared, and properly varied to suit the text they introduce.

16. In a Mass with the people the readings are always to be proclaimed at the ambo.
18. At the conclusion of the other readings, *The word of the Lord* may be sung, even by someone other than the reader; all respond with the acclamation. In this way the assembled congregation pays reverence to the word of God it has listened to in faith and gratitude.
28. The Liturgy of the Word must be celebrated in a way that fosters meditation; clearly, any sort of haste that hinders recollection must be avoided. The dialogue between God and his people taking place through the Holy Spirit demands short intervals of silence, suited to the assembled congregation, as an opportunity to take the word of God to heart and to prepare a response to it in prayer.
Proper times for silence during the Liturgy of the Word are, for example, before this Liturgy begins, after the first and the second reading, after the homily.

Third Instruction on the Correct Implementation of the Constitution on the Sacred Liturgy

2. The Holy Scriptures, of all the texts proclaimed in the liturgical assembly, are of the greatest value: in the readings, God speaks to His people, and Christ, present in His word, announces the good news of the Gospel. Therefore:
    (a) Full importance must be given to the Liturgy of the Word in the Mass. Other readings, whether from sacred or profane authors of past or present, may never be substituted for the Word of God, nor may only a single Scripture lesson be read …
    (b) The Liturgy of the Word prepares the assembly and leads them to the celebration of the Eucharist. Thus the two parts of the Mass form one act of worship and may not be celebrated separately, at different times or in different places.

Music in Catholic Worship

45. Readings from scripture are the heart of the liturgy of the word. The homily, responsorial psalms, profession of faith, and general intercessions develop and complete it. In the readings, God speaks to his people and nourishes their spirit; Christ is present through his word. The homily explains the readings. The chants and the profession of faith comprise the people's acceptance of God's Word. It is of primary importance that the people hear God's message of love, digest it with the aid of psalms, silence and the homily, and respond, involving themselves in the great covenant of love and redemption. All else is secondary.

Reflection

The purpose of the Liturgy of the Word is not to communicate information about God and the works of God. It is to forge a common identity and spirituality based upon the action of God among God's people today. Its goal is to touch, move, and transform hearts, doing so by a dynamic blend of proclaiming, listening, responding, meditating, and being silent. "In the readings, explained by the homily, God is speaking to his people, opening up to them the mystery of redemption and salvation, and nourishing their spirit; Christ himself is present in the midst of the faithful through his own word" (GIRM no. 55). It is Christ himself "who speaks when the holy Scriptures are read in the Church" (Constitution on the Sacred Liturgy, *Sacrosanctum Concilium*, art. 7). As Christ is present in the Eucharist to give himself as food, he is present also when the Scriptures are proclaimed to offer his message of redemption and to arouse faith in those who hear his message. "Faith, then, comes through hearing, and what is heard is the word of Christ" (Romans 10:17).

All Christian liturgy includes as core elements both the proclamation of the word of God and common prayer. The Liturgy of the Word, then, is not just a preparation for the celebration of the Eucharist. A profound relationship exists between the two since the word of God and the bread of life are two aspects of the same mystery. "The Church has always venerated the divine Scriptures just as she venerates the body of the Lord, since from the table of both the word of God and of the body of Christ she unceasingly receives and offers to the faithful the bread of life, especially in the sacred liturgy" (Constitution on Divine Revelation, *Dei Verbum*, art. 21). Jesus is the living Word, the revelation of the Father. He is also the Bread of Life, the nourishment of his people. The Liturgy of the Word and the Liturgy of the Eucharist "form but one single act of worship" (Constitution on the Sacred Liturgy, *Sacrosanctum Concilium*, art. 56).

Suggested Questions for Discussion

1. What is the purpose of the Liturgy of the Word?
2. In what way can it be called a celebration?
3. How may a community, before the liturgy itself, prepare its members for the Liturgy of the Word?
4. What responsibilities do those who proclaim the word have to themselves as proclaimers? To the members of the community? To God?
5. What is the difference between a reading and a proclamation?
6. Are all the readings proclaimed from one lectern or ambo?
7. What should be the physical characteristics of the Lectionary/Book of the Gospels?
8. Where is the Lectionary placed before and after the readings?
9. Why are the readings to be proclaimed from the Lectionary/Book of the Gospels rather than from a participation aid?
10. When is it appropriate to have an introduction to a reading? What should be the nature and length of such introductions? By whom should they be given?
11. Is it appropriate to raise the book on high at the conclusion of a reading?
12. Would it not be better if communities could choose the Scriptural passages according to their own needs?

13. May non-biblical readings ever be used in the celebration? Why may they not replace the appointed Scriptural texts?
14. On such occasions as days of recollection, is it appropriate to extend the Liturgy of the Word by a long period of prayer and reflection and then to conclude with the Liturgy of the Eucharist?
15. Is it ever allowed to use one location for the Liturgy of the Word and another for the liturgy of the eucharist?
16. When and how are late-comers seated?

12
First Reading

Historical Survey

An integral and primary element of the Jewish synagogue service was the reading of the Law and the Prophets. The books of Moses were read continuously from one session to another; the lesson from the Prophets was usually selected at will. This Jewish tradition as well as the conviction that all the Scriptures are God's inspired word resulted in the presence of at least one Old Testament reading in the early Christian Liturgy of the Word. At Rome, it would seem, this reading was followed by two New Testament selections, the second always being the Gospel. Before long and for reasons unknown the first reading was omitted. As a result of this and other changes, most of the Old Testament selections occurred only on weekdays and thus were not heard by the majority of the faithful. To allow for a greater familiarity of the faithful with the Old Testament, the Second Vatican Council expressed the wish that "the treasures of the Bible … be opened up more lavishly, so that a richer fare may be provided for the faithful at the table of God's Word" (Constitution on the Sacred Liturgy, *Sacrosanctum Concilium,* art. 51).

On Sundays and major feasts there are always three readings. The first is usually taken from the Old Testament. As a rule, the Old Testament texts were chosen to prepare for the Gospel, following such principles as prophecy-fulfillment or thematic continuity/contrast. In keeping with ancient tradition the first reading during the Easter season is taken from the Acts of the Apostles which show how the early Church gave witness to the Paschal Mystery.

On weekdays (except in the case of a Solemnity) there is only one reading before the Gospel. During Advent and Lent the first is always from the Old Testament and is related to the Gospel. Within Ordinary Time selections from both Old and New Testaments appear, but no attempt was made to harmonize this reading with the Gospel.

Documentation

General Instruction of the Roman Missal, Third Typical Edition

128. After the Collect, all sit. The priest may, very briefly, introduce the faithful to the Liturgy of the Word. Then the lector goes to the ambo and, from the Lectionary already placed there before Mass, proclaims the first reading, to which all listen. At the end, the lector says the acclamation *Verbum Domini (The word of the Lord),* and all respond, *Deo gratias (Thanks be to God).*

    Then, as appropriate, a few moments of silence may be observed so that all may meditate on what they have heard.

45. Sacred silence also, as part of the celebration, is to be observed at the designated times. Its purpose, however, depends on the time it occurs in each part of the celebration. Thus … at the conclusion of a reading or the homily, all meditate briefly on what they have heard …

Reflection

The presence of the Old Testament reading manifests the Church's firm conviction that all Scripture is the word of God. There is a continuity between the two Testaments: both lead the congregation to Jesus Christ. As St. Augustine (354–430) so succinctly stated it, "In the Old Testament the New is hidden, in the New Testament the Old appears." And according to St. Irenaeus, Bishop of Lyons (c.130–c.200), "The writings of Moses are the words of Christ."

Suggested Questions for Discussion

1. What is the purpose of the first reading?
2. What are the advantages and/or disadvantages of always having three readings on Sundays?
3. What are the advantages and/or disadvantages of having a thematic connection between the readings?
4. Should the lector bow before the altar as he or she approaches the ambo?
5. In what manner does the lector approach the ambo? When does the reading begin?
6. Where does the lector sit when not proclaiming the reading? In the sanctuary or elsewhere? Why?
7. Does a short period of silence ever follow or precede the reading?

13
Responsorial Psalm

Historical Survey

Continuing the practice of the Jewish synagogue, Christians traditionally sang a psalm or biblical canticle after the first reading. At Rome a cantor or subdeacon approached the ambo. He stood on one of its lower steps *(gradus)* and began the chant which was eventually called the gradual. The psalm verses were sung by the soloist, and the people responded with a short refrain which was frequently taken from the psalm itself. Once florid melodies evolved, the psalm text was abbreviated, and the singing was done by a trained body of singers.

Today the responsorial psalm has been restored to a place of special importance. Normatively it is sung, and the whole assembly participates by singing the response. Very frequently the psalm has a textual or spiritual relationship to one of the readings. At times psalms traditional to certain seasons, e.g., Psalms 118 and 66 for Easter, are used. Where no special thematic or liturgical relationship to the scriptural texts or season appears, the lectionary appoints certain other psalms so that the assembly may make contact with the psalter as a whole. To facilitate the singing of the psalms, the lectionary also appoints a number of common psalms and refrains which may be used throughout different liturgical seasons.

Documentation

General Instruction of the Roman Missal, Third Typical Edition

61. After the first reading comes the responsorial Psalm, which is an integral part of the Liturgy of the Word and holds great liturgical and pastoral importance, because it fosters meditation on the word of God.

    The responsorial Psalm should correspond to each reading and should, as a rule, be taken from the Lectionary.

    It is preferable that the responsorial Psalm be sung, at least as far as the people's response is concerned. Hence, the psalmist, or the cantor of the Psalm, sings the verses of the Psalm from the ambo or another suitable place. The entire congregation remains seated and listens but, as a rule, takes part by singing the response, except when the Psalm is sung straight through without a response. In order, however, that the people may be able to sing the Psalm response more readily, texts of some responses and Psalms have been chosen for the various seasons of the year or for the various categories of Saints. These may be used in place of the text corresponding to the reading whenever the Psalm is sung. If the Psalm cannot be sung, then it should be recited in such a way that it is particularly suited to fostering meditation on the word of God.

In the dioceses of the United States of America, the following may also be sung in place of the Psalm assigned in the *Lectionary for Mass*: either the proper or seasonal antiphon and Psalm from the *Lectionary*, as found either in the *Roman Gradual* or *Simple Gradual* or in another musical setting; or an antiphon and Psalm from another collection of the psalms and antiphons, including psalms arranged in metrical form, providing that they have been approved by the United States Conference of Catholic Bishops or the Diocesan Bishop. Songs or hymns may not be used in place of the responsorial Psalm.

129. Then the psalmist or even a lector proclaims the verses of the psalm and the people sing or say the response as usual.

Lectionary for Mass: Introduction

19. The responsorial psalm, also called the gradual, has great liturgical and pastoral significance because it is an "integral part of the liturgy of the word." Accordingly, the faithful must be continually instructed on the way to perceive the word of God speaking in the psalms and to turn these psalms into the prayer of the Church. This, of course, "will be achieved more readily if a deeper understanding of the psalms, according to the meaning with which they are sung in the sacred Liturgy, is more diligently promoted among the clergy and communicated to all the faithful by means of appropriate catechesis."
Brief remarks about the choice of the psalm and response as well as their correspondence to the readings may be helpful.

20. As a rule the responsorial psalm should be sung. There are two established ways of singing the psalm after the first reading: responsorially and directly. In responsorial singing, which, as far as possible, is to be given preference, the psalmist, or cantor of the psalm, sings the psalm verse and the whole congregation joins in by singing the response. In direct singing of the psalm there is no intervening response by the community; either the psalmist, or cantor of the psalm, sings the psalm alone as the community listens or else all sing it together.

21. The singing of the psalm, or even of the response alone, is a great help toward understanding and meditating on the psalm's spiritual meaning. To foster the congregation's singing, every means available in each individual culture is to be employed. In particular, use is to be made of all the relevant options provided in the Order of Readings for Mass regarding responses corresponding to the different liturgical seasons.

22. When not sung, the psalm after the reading is to be recited in a manner conducive to meditation on the word of God.
The responsorial psalm is sung or recited by the psalmist or cantor at the ambo.

Music in Catholic Worship

63. This unique and very important song is the response to the first lesson. The new lectionary's determination to match the content of the psalms to the theme of the reading is reflected in its listing of 900 refrains. The

liturgy of the Word comes more fully to life if between the first two readings a cantor sings the psalm and all sing the response. Since most groups cannot learn a new response every week, seasonal refrains are offered in the lectionary itself and in the *Simple Gradual*. Other psalms and refrains may also be used, including psalms arranged in responsorial form and metrical and similar versions of psalms, provided they are used in accordance with the principles of the *Simple Gradual* and are selected in harmony with the liturgical season, feast or occasion. The choice of the texts which are not from the psalter is not extended to the chants between the readings (NCCB, November 1968; cf. GIRM 6). To facilitate reflection, there may be a brief period of silence between the first reading and the responsorial psalm.

Reflection

The responsorial psalm, the only psalm used in the Mass for its own sake and not to accompany some particular action, is not just a response to the reading. It helps the gathered assembly create an atmosphere of prayer, one in which all can recall what God has done and continues to do. To a certain extent the psalm serves as a meditative prolongation of the reading, offering us through poetry a rich opportunity to savor the word of God.

Suggested Questions for Discussion

1. What is the purpose of the psalm response?
2. In what way may it be considered a continuation of the first reading?
3. Are the people generally aware of the reason why a particular psalm is used?
4. May a non biblical text ever replace the psalm? May another scriptural text, not taken from the Psalter, ever replace the psalm?
5. What is the nature of the psalm when it is not sung?
6. Who sings the psalm verses? From where?
7. What part does the whole gathered assembly play in the psalm response?
8. If not sung, may the psalm be replaced by a period of silence?

14
Second Reading

Historical Survey

For centuries the Roman Liturgy used the term "Epistle" to designate the reading which preceded the Gospel even when this reading was not taken from a New Testament letter. In the east, however, the reading before the Gospel was simply called "the Apostle," a designation suitable for all the books of the New Testament which come down to us from the Church of the Apostles.

Today a New Testament text is always given as the second reading on Sundays and Solemnities. Although the choice of the text was made quite independently of the first reading or the Gospel, during certain seasons passages have been selected to correspond with the mystery being celebrated at a particular time of the liturgical year. For example, during the Christmas season there is a successive reading from the First Letter of St. John which recounts the mystery of love made incarnate in Christ.

Documentation

General Instruction of the Roman Missal, Third Typical Edition

130. If there is to be a second reading before the Gospel, the lector proclaims it from the ambo. All listen and at the end respond with the acclamation. … Then, as appropriate, a few moments of silence may be observed.
45. Sacred silence also, as part of the celebration, must be observed at the designated times. Its purpose, however, depends on the time it occurs in each part of the celebration. Thus … at the conclusion of a reading or the homily, all meditate briefly on what they have heard …

Reflection

In the second reading the congregation often encounters the early Church living its Christian faith. The witness of the apostolic community provides an example for all time since Christians of every age are to recall the love of the Father enfleshed in Christ, the good news of redemption, the duty of Christian love. All followers of Jesus are to live decently and without blemish, to be tolerant of one another, to be steadfast in the faith.

Suggested Questions for Discussion

1. What is the purpose of the second reading?
2. Are two lectors used when there are two readings before the gospel?
3. Does a period of silence ever follow the second reading?
4. Where is the Lectionary placed after the second reading?

15
Alleluia/Gospel Acclamation; Sequence

Historical Survey

The Hebrew "Halleluiah" (rendered in Latin and Greek as "Alleluia") means "Praise YHWH" (the Hebrew letters for the divine name, never pronounced aloud in Judaism out of a profound respect for its holiness) or "Praise the Lord." In the Old Testament this joyful cry appears at the beginning or end of certain psalms that are thought to have been intended for use in the Temple liturgy. The only occurrence of the alleluia in the New Testament appears in the Book of Revelation (19:1–9) where it forms part of the victory hymn sung by the redeemed in heaven.

The introduction of the alleluia into the liturgy of the west posed an initial problem as to the occasion of its use. According to St. Augustine (354–430) it was sung every Sunday, but in fifth-century Rome, where it was perhaps introduced under eastern influence, it was sung only on Easter. Roman practice eventually extended its use to the whole Paschal season and then throughout the liturgical year except during Lent. The acclamation was linked to the Gospel (yet its verse was not necessarily taken from the Gospel) and often accompanied a procession with the Gospel book. This practice has now been restored, with the verse for Sundays often being taken from the Gospels. During the week texts from the Book of Psalms and other Scriptural writings are also found.

At an early period soloists were accustomed to ornament the final syllable of the alleluia with the *jubilus*, a long musical extension described by St. Augustine as "joy without words." In the early Middle Ages words were set to these vocalizations, and this in turn gave rise in Germanic countries to the composition of numerous sequences, i.e., somewhat independent musical compositions, often having rhymed texts, which immediately followed the alleluia. Over five thousand of these compositions existed in the Middle Ages. Their melodies were quite simple, thereby encouraging popular singing. The number of such pieces used in the liturgy was greatly reduced in the sixteenth century. Today the Sequence is obligatory on Easter and Pentecost; it may be used on the Solemnity of the Most Holy Body and Blood of the Lord and the optional Memorial of Our Lady of Sorrows.

Because of its Paschal connotations the alleluia was not used during the season of Lent when it was replaced by a psalm chant known as the tract, i.e., a solo chant sung all the way through without any repetition. Still omitted during Lent, the alleluia is usually replaced by an equivalent acclamation of praise. The alleluia or its equivalent is followed by a verse, often taken from the following Gospel reading. The acclamation is repeated after this verse.

Documentation

General Instruction of the Roman Missal, Third Typical Edition

62. After the reading that immediately precedes the Gospel, the *Alleluia* or another chant indicated by the rubrics is sung, as required by the liturgical season. An acclamation of this kind constitutes a rite or act in itself, by which the assembly of the faithful welcomes and greets the Lord who is about to speak to them in the Gospel and professes its faith by means of the chant. It is sung by all while standing and is led by the choir or a cantor, being repeated if this is appropriate. The verse, however, is sung either by the choir or by the cantor.
    a) The Alleluia is sung in every season other than Lent. The verses are taken from the Lectionary or the Graduale.
    b) During Lent, in place of the *Alleluia*, the verse before the Gospel is sung, as indicated in the Lectionary. It is also permissible to sing another psalm or tract, as found in the *Graduale*.

63. When there is only one reading before the Gospel,
    a) During a season when the *Alleluia* is to be said, either the *Alleluia* Psalm or the responsorial Psalm followed by the *Alleluia* with its verse may be used;
    b) During the season when the *Alleluia* is not to be said, either the psalm and the verse before the Gospel or the psalm alone may be used;
    c) The *Alleluia* or verse before the Gospel may be omitted if they are not sung.

64. The Sequence, which is optional except on Easter Sunday and on Pentecost Day, is sung before the *Alleluia*.

43. The faithful should stand … for the *Alleluia* chant before the Gospel …

Lectionary for Mass: Introduction

23. The Alleluia or, as the liturgical season requires, the verse before the Gospel, is also a "rite or act standing by itself." It serves as the greeting of welcome of the assembled faithful to the Lord who is about to speak to them and as an expression of their faith through song.
    The Alleluia or the verse before the Gospel must be sung and during it all stand. It is not to be sung only by the cantor who intones it or by the choir, but by the whole of the people together.

Music in Catholic Worship

55. This acclamation of paschal joy is both a reflection upon the Word of God proclaimed in the Liturgy and a preparation for the gospel. All stand to sing it. After the cantor or choir sings the alleluia(s), the people customarily repeat it. Then a single proper verse is sung by the cantor or choir, and all repeat the alleluia(s). If not sung, the alleluia should be omitted. (GIRM 39 [63]. The first edition of *Music in Catholic Worship* had the word "may" instead of "should." This change has been made in the second edition in light of the recent norm found in *The Lectionary for Mass*, Introduction {second typical edition, 1981} 23: "The Alleluia or the verse before the Gospel must be sung and during it, all stand. It is not to be sung by the cantor who intones it or by the choir, but by the whole congregation together.") A moment

of silent reflection may be observed in its place. During Lent a brief verse of acclamatory character replaces the alleluia and is sung in the same way.

Reflection

It has often been said that the alleluia is the victory song of a Paschal people. In the words attributed to St. Augustine, "We are an Easter people, and alleluia is our song." Used as the Gospel Acclamation, the Alleluia accompanies the Gospel procession during which the whole liturgical assembly praises Christ who comes to proclaim the good news of salvation. The acclamation is to be sung; when not sung, it is to be omitted. The people stand to express their readiness for the Gospel reading.

Suggested Questions for Discussion

1. What is the purpose of the Gospel acclamation?
2. When does it begin?
3. Why is it to be sung?
4. How is the acclamation introduced musically?
5. What is the purpose of the verse? Is it to be recited?
6. How can the special Paschal character of the alleluia be expressed during the Easter season?
7. Does the special Paschal significance of the alleluia appear when it is sung throughout most of the year?
8. Since every celebration of the Eucharist is a celebration of the Paschal Mystery, why is the Alleluia omitted during Lent?
9. What is the purpose of the sequence?

16 Gospel

Historical Survey

From earliest times the primacy of the Gospel has been emphasized by special signs of respect and honor surrounding its liturgical proclamation. Whereas the other readings could be proclaimed by any lector, a special minister was appointed to read the Gospel. Traditionally this was the deacon who was considered the special exemplar of Christ the servant. Only in the absence of a deacon did a priest proclaim the Gospel.

In almost all liturgies of east and west the Gospel book was brought in procession to the ambo. The custom of carrying candles and incense in the procession probably derives from court usage where it was a means of showing respect to a ruler appearing in public. Although the people were seated for the other readings, as early as the fourth century in the east they began to stand for the Gospel as a sign of respect and alertness in the presence of the Risen Lord.

The Middle Ages witnessed the development of additional honorific signs. The making of small signs of the cross on the book, forehead, mouth and heart was seen as expressing readiness to open one's mind to the word, to confess it with the mouth, and to safeguard it in the heart. In eighth-century Rome the book was kissed by all the clergy after the proclamation. Occasionally it was even given to the whole congregation to kiss. Eventually this gesture was reserved to the presiding priest or Bishop. Formulas such as "May the words of the Gospel wipe away our sins" to accompany the kiss appear from about the year 1000. Acclamations addressed to Christ at the beginning and end of the Gospel proclamation date from Carolingian times. By the eleventh century the book itself was incensed. The Order of Mass retains many such beautiful signs of solemnity and veneration.

The use of a special book for the proclamation of the Gospel has a long tradition in the Church. Initially the Scripture passages for the day were read from a copy of the New Testament with marginal notes indicating the day and with a cross indicating the beginning of the reading. Soon lists or indexes of readings were placed at the end (or at times the beginning) of the New Testament codex. These indicated the day, the New Testament book, and the beginning and ending of the passage to be read. There were also books that contained according to the liturgical calendar the full texts of the individual readings, some books (called epistolaries) with only the first readings, other books (evangeliaries, evangelistaries, namely Gospel books) with only the Gospel reading, and still other volumes (especially after the year 1000) containing the full texts of both readings. The Gospel book in particular was highly ornamented with gold and silver and adorned with precious stones—truly, a sight to behold! Often coexisting with one another and designated by a large variety of names, these books eventually gave way to what is known as the Missal, namely, one book containing all the texts of the Mass. Today the

Lectionary containing the readings is usually been printed once again as a separate book.

Our present Book of the Gospels reintroduces us to a liturgical tradition that visually tells us that the Gospel is a special part of God's holy word, for it contains in a unique way the incarnate Word himself speaking to us. The procession with this book has also been restored. Whether solemn or simple in form, there is a Gospel procession in every celebration.

Documentation

General Instruction of the Roman Missal, Third Typical Edition

60. The reading of the Gospel is the high point of the Liturgy of the Word. The Liturgy itself teaches that great reverence is to be shown to it by setting it off from the other readings with special marks of honor: whether on the part of the minister appointed to proclaim it prepares himself by a blessing or prayer; or on the part of the faithful, who stand as they listen to it being read and through their acclamations acknowledge and confess Christ present and speaking to them; or by the very marks of reverence are given to the Book of the Gospels.

132. During the singing of the Alleluia or other chant, if incense is used, the priest puts some into the thurible and blesses it. Then, with hands joined, he bows profoundly before the altar and quietly says, *Munda cor meum (May the word of the gospel wipe away our sins)*.

133. If the Book of the Gospels is on the altar, the priest then takes it and goes to the ambo, carrying the Book of the Gospels slightly elevated and preceded by the lay ministers, who may carry the thurible and the candles. Those present turn towards the ambo as a sign of special reverence to the Gospel of Christ.

134. At the ambo, the priest opens the book and, with hands joined, says, *Dominus vobiscum (The Lord be with you)*, and the people respond, *Et cum spiritu tuo (And also with you)*. Then he says, *Lectio sancti Evangelii (A reading from the holy Gospel)*, making the sign of the cross with his thumb on the book and on his forehead, mouth, and breast, which everyone else does as well. The people say the acclamation *Gloria tibi, Domine (Glory to you, Lord)*. The priest incenses the book, if incense is used (cf. below, nos. 276-277). Then he proclaims the Gospel and at the end says the acclamation *Verbum Domini (The Gospel of the Lord)*, to which all respond, *Laus tibi, Christe (Praise to you, Lord Jesus Christ)*. The priest kisses the book, saying quietly, *Per evangelica dicta (May the words of the gospel)*.

276. Thurification or incensation is an expression of reverence and of prayer, as is signified in Sacred Scripture (cf. Ps 141 [140]:2, Rev 8:3).

    Incense may be used if desired in any form of Mass …

    c) At the Gospel procession and the proclamation of the Gospel itself …

277. The priest, having put incense into the thurible, blesses it with the sign of the Cross, without saying anything.

    Before and after an incensation, a profound bow is made to the person or object that is incensed, except for the incensation of the altar and the offerings for the Sacrifice of the Mass.

The following are incensed with three swings of the thurible: … the Book of the Gospels …

Lectionary for Mass: Introduction

17. Of all the rites connected with the Liturgy of the Word, the reverence due to the Gospel reading must receive special attention. Where there is an Evangeliary or Book of Gospels that has been carried in by the deacon or reader during the entry procession, it is most fitting that the deacon or a priest, when there is no deacon, take the book from the altar and carry it to the ambo. He is preceded by servers with candles and incense or other symbols of reverence that may be customary. As the faithful stand and acclaim the Lord, they show honor to the Book of Gospels. The deacon who is to read the Gospel, bowing in front of the one presiding, asks and receives the blessing. When no deacon is present, the priest, bowing before the altar, prays inaudibly, Almighty God, cleanse my heart …
At the ambo the one who proclaims the Gospel greets the people, who are standing, and announces the reading as he makes the sign of the cross on forehead, mouth, and breast. If incense is used, he next incenses the book, then reads the Gospel. When finished, he kisses the book, saying the appointed words inaudibly.
Even if the Gospel itself is not sung, it is appropriate for the greeting The Lord be with you, and A reading from the holy Gospel according to … and at the end The Gospel of the Lord to be sung, in order that the congregation may also sing its acclamations. This is a way both of bringing out the importance of the Gospel reading and of stirring up the faith of those who hear it.

Reflection

Special signs of solemnity surround the Gospel proclamation since this reading is the high point of the Liturgy of the Word. The Good News of salvation, a living word, is proclaimed by the Risen Lord. It is Christ present among his own who continues to speak to his people as he calls them to faith and conversion.

Suggested Questions for Discussion

1. What is the purpose of the Gospel procession?
2. Why are special signs of solemnity given only to the Gospel?
3. On what occasions is a more solemn procession appropriate?
4. How can the procession be made more solemn?
5. What is the function of the initial "The Lord be with you"?
6. Should a gesture accompany these words?
7. Do people understand the meaning of the sign of the cross? Is it appropriate for the whole assembly to make this sign?
8. What is the meaning of the phrase "May the words of the Gospel wipe away our sins"?
9. Where is the Book of the Gospels placed after the Gospel proclamation?

17 Homily

Historical Survey

In the synagogue service the readings from the Law and the Prophets were concluded by an explanation given by one of those present. One of the oldest descriptions of the Eucharist attests the same practice. Writing about the year 150, Justin the Martyr says that after the readings the Bishop instructed and exhorted the people to imitate the things they heard (see *I Apologia 67:4*). Like the Eucharist itself, the bread of God's word was to be broken, to be applied to the concrete life situations of the people. In some areas of the east, when several priests were present, each of them would preach after the readings and then the Bishop himself would do so. The numerous homilies (the word "homily" comes from the Greek for instruction or informal discourse) that have come down to us from the patristic period, e.g., those of St. John Chrysostom (c.347–407), St. Augustine (354–430), St. Leo the Great (d.461), witness a strong homiletic tradition. Two characteristics mark this tradition: the theme is selected from the day's readings or another part of the celebration; the type of speech is somewhat informal, lacking oratorical style and designed to elicit a response from the people.

Although a certain enthusiasm for preaching existed during the Middle Ages, the nature of the homily as a living application of God's proclaimed word was not always given great emphasis. Sometimes a preacher might read a homily from one of the Fathers. Often an explanation on the Our Father, the Creed, or the Commandments was given. Preaching was often considered as extrinsic to the liturgy with the preacher, having removed his maniple, beginning and concluding his preaching with the sign of the cross. It is true that the late Middle Ages saw a revival of preaching by the mendicant orders, but this usually took place apart from the Mass.

The Second Vatican Council underlined the importance of the homily and emphasized it as an integral part of the Liturgy. "By means of the homily the mysteries of the faith and the guiding principles of the Christian life are expounded from the sacred text during the course of the liturgical year; the homily, therefore, is to be highly esteemed as part of the liturgy itself; in fact, at those Masses which are celebrated with the assistance of the people on Sundays and feasts of obligation, it should not be omitted except for a serious reason" (Constitution on the Sacred Liturgy, art. 52).

Documentation

General Instruction of the Roman Missal, Third Typical Edition

65. The homily is part of the Liturgy and is strongly recommended, for it is necessary for the nurturing of the Christian life. It should be an exposition of some aspect of the readings from Sacred Scripture or of another text

from the Ordinary or from the Proper of the Mass of the day and should take into account both the mystery being celebrated and the particular needs of the listeners.

66. The Homily should ordinarily be given by the priest celebrant himself. He may entrust it to a concelebrating priest or occasionally, according to circumstances, to the deacon, but never to a lay person. In particular cases and for a just cause, the homily may even be given by a Bishop or a priest who is present at the celebration but cannot concelebrate.

   There is to be a homily on Sundays and holy days of obligation at all Masses that are celebrated with the participation of a congregation; it may not be omitted without a serious reason. It is recommended on other days, especially on the weekdays of Advent, Lent, and the Easter Season, as well as on other festive days and occasions when the people come to church in greater numbers.

   After the homily a brief period of silence is appropriately observed.

45. Sacred silence also, as part of the celebration, is to be observed at the designated times. Its purpose, however, depends on the time it occurs in each part of the celebration. Thus … at the conclusion of a reading or the homily, all meditate briefly on what they have heard …

136. The priest, standing at the chair or at the ambo itself or, when appropriate, in another suitable place, gives the homily. When the homily is completed, a period of silence may be observed.

Lectionary for Mass: Introduction

24. Through the course of the liturgical year the homily sets forth the mysteries of faith and the standards of the Christian life on the basis of the sacred text. Beginning with the Constitution on the Liturgy, the homily as part of the Liturgy of the Word has been repeatedly and strongly recommended and in some cases it is obligatory. As a rule it is to be given by the one presiding. The purpose of the homily at Mass is that the spoken word of God and the Liturgy of the Eucharist may together become "a proclamation of God's wonderful works in the history of salvation, the mystery of Christ." Through the readings and homily Christ's paschal mystery is proclaimed; through the sacrifice of the Mass it becomes present. Moreover Christ himself is always present and active in the preaching of his Church.

   Whether the homily explains the text of the Sacred Scriptures proclaimed in the readings or some other text of the Liturgy, it must always lead the community of the faithful to celebrate the Eucharist actively, "so that they may hold fast in their lives to what they have grasped by faith." From this living explanation, the word of God proclaimed in the readings and the Church's celebration of the day's Liturgy will have greater impact. But this demands that the homily be truly the fruit of meditation, carefully prepared, neither too long nor too short, and suited to all those present, even children and the uneducated.

   At a concelebration, the celebrant or one of the concelebrants as a rule gives the homily.

25. On the prescribed days, that is, Sundays and holy days of obligation, there must be a homily in all Masses celebrated with a congregation, even Masses on the preceding evening; the homily may not be omitted without a serious reason. There is also to be a homily in Masses with children and with special groups.

    A homily is strongly recommended on the weekdays of Advent, Lent, and the Easter season for the sake of the faithful who regularly take part in the celebration of Mass; also on other feasts and occasions when a large congregation is present.

26. The priest celebrant gives the homily, standing either at the chair or at the ambo.

27. Any necessary announcements are to be kept completely separate from the homily; they must take place following the prayer after Communion.

Third Instruction on the Correct Implementation of the Constitution on the Sacred Liturgy

2a. … The purpose of the homily is to explain the readings and make them relevant for the present day. This is the task of the priest, and the faithful should not add comments or engage in dialogue during the homily.

Reflection

The homily, an integral part of the Liturgy of the Word, is a continuation of God's saving message which elicits faith and conversion. It is neither exegesis nor moral exhortation but a joyful proclamation of God's saving deeds in Christ. Basing his preaching on the liturgical texts, the homilist breaks the bread of God's word by actualizing it, by showing how God is continuing to act and speak among his people today. Doing so, the homilist is never forgetful of St. Augustine's admonition that the speaker is to instruct, to teach, and to charm. Christianity is a religion that tells a story, and it is by hearing this story that the members of the liturgical assembly are called to become a holy people so that they can better celebrate the Eucharist and offer themselves with and through Christ in the Eucharistic Prayer.

Suggested Questions for Discussion

1. What is the purpose of the homily?
2. What is the difference between a homily and a sermon?
3. How often is the homily an actualization of the readings?
4. Need the homily be based on all the readings?
5. Should representative members of the community be offered an opportunity to help the homilist in his preparation?
6. By whom and from where is the homily to be given?
7. Why are comments, dialogue, etc. forbidden?
8. Is it correct to begin and end the homily with "In the name of the Father and of …"?
9. Does a period of silence ever follow the homily?

18
Profession of Faith

Historical Survey

In early Christianity the Profession of Faith was primarily associated with Baptism. The candidate went down into the water and was required to confess personal belief by responding to a series of questions dealing with the three Persons of the Trinity. After each question and answer the person was immersed. As the catechumenate developed, the candidates finished their preparation for the Sacrament by memorizing a credal formula and reciting it back to the Bishop prior to the baptismal celebration. This is the distant origin of what is known as the Apostles' Creed, a profession of faith which, according to pious legend, was a joint composition by the twelve Apostles. The date of its present text is not earlier than the beginning of the sixth century.

The Creed professed at Mass, however, is a summary of the faith expressed by the Councils of Nicaea (325) and of Constantinople (381) as ratified by the Council of Chalcedon (451). In the east it entered the Mass in the early part of the sixth century, most often before the Eucharistic Prayer. Toward the end of the same century the Creed appeared in Spain where it was chanted before the Lord's Prayer. From there it spread to Ireland where it served to conclude the Liturgy of the Word. Under the influence of Charlemagne its use spread throughout the Carolingian empire. In 1014 Emperor Henry II arrived at Rome for his coronation and expressed surprise that the Creed was missing from the Mass as celebrated in that city. Pope Benedict VII thereupon included it in the Roman Mass on all Sundays and on those feasts mentioned in the Creed. In following centuries its use was extended to other festive occasions.

The Order of Mass retains the Profession of Faith on Sundays and solemnities, although it may also be used on especially festive occasions. The *Missale Romanum*, Third Edition, allows both the Nicene Creed and the Apostles' Creed to be used as a response of faith on the part of the community.

Documentation

General Instruction of the Roman Missal, Third Typical Edition

67. The purpose of the *Symbolum* or Profession of Faith, or Creed, is that the whole gathered people may respond to the word of God proclaimed in the readings taken from Sacred Scripture and explained in the homily and that they may also call to mind and confess the great mysteries of the faith by reciting the rule of faith in a formula approved for liturgical use, before these mysteries are celebrated in the Eucharist.

68. The Creed is to be sung or said by the priest together with the people on Sundays and Solemnities. It may be said also at particular celebrations of a more solemn character.

    If it is sung, it is begun by the priest or, if this is appropriate, by a cantor or by the choir. It is sung, however, either by all together or by the people alternating with the choir.

    If not sung, it is to be recited by all together or by two parts of the assembly responding one to the other.

137. The Creed is sung or recited by the priest together with the people (cf. above, no. 68) with everyone standing. At the words *et incarnatus est (by the power of the Holy Spirit ... became man)* all make a profound bow; but on the Solemnities of the Annunciation and of the Nativity of the Lord, all genuflect.

43. The faithful should stand ... during the Profession of Faith ...

Lectionary for Mass: Introduction

29. The symbol, creed, or profession of faith, said when the rubrics require, has as its purpose in the celebration of Mass that the assembled congregation may respond and give assent to the word of God heard in the readings and through the homily, and that before beginning to celebrate in the Eucharist the mystery of faith it may call to mind the rule of faith in a formulary approved by the Church.

Music in Catholic Worship

69. This is a communal profession of faith in which " ... the people who have heard the Word of God in the lesson and in the homily may assent and respond to it, and may renew in themselves the rule of faith as they begin to celebrate the Eucharist." (GIRM 43 [67]) It is usually preferable that the Creed be spoken in declamatory fashion rather than sung. If it is sung, it might more effectively take the form of a simple musical declamation rather than an extensive and involved musical structure.

Reflection

The Creed is a corporate profession of faith whereby the community responds, assents, and adheres to the word of God proclaimed in the Scriptures and preached in the homily. It is a response not only to doctrinal propositions but also to the person of Christ present in the word. At the same time the profession links the Liturgies of the Word and Eucharist as the congregation recalls the mysteries of faith which will again be proclaimed in the Eucharistic Prayer. The people accept God's word before they more on to the celebration of the Eucharist, which itself is a profession of faith.

Suggested Questions for Discussion

1. What is the purpose of the Profession of Faith as part of the Liturgy?
2. What is the particular value of the Nicene Creed as a profession of faith within the Liturgy?
3. What is the particular value of the Apostles' Creed as a profession of faith within the Liturgy?

4. Can the Profession of Faith be experienced as a vibrant expression of belief when it is read from a participation aid?
5. What does the Profession of Faith contribute to the special solemnity of Sundays and certain feasts?
6. Is it preferable to sing or to recite the Profession of Faith?
7. When recited, may it be proclaimed in alternation?
8. Who begins the Creed?
9. May the Creed be replaced by a hymn?

19
Prayer of the Faithful

Historical Survey

One of the components of the synagogue liturgy was a series of eighteen blessings containing requests for individual and universal needs. At a very early period a similar prayer became a fixed part of the Liturgy in both east and west. St. Justin the Martyr, writing in mid-second century Rome, describes the celebration of Baptism and then adds that all "offer prayers in common for ourselves, for him who had just been enlightened, and for people everywhere" (*I Apologia 65:1*). Justin goes on to describe the Eucharist which followed. So significant were these prayers that the catechumens could not be present for them and thus were dismissed beforehand. A remnant of the ancient form of this prayer at Rome is found in the Solemn Prayers of Good Friday. But with the introduction from the east of a litanic form of supplication and due to a number of unfortunate liturgical reforms whose details are simply lost in history, these prayers, except on Good Friday, disappeared from the Roman Mass till restored in their litanic form by the Second Vatican Council.

These are officially called the Prayer of the Faithful since, as already mentioned, in ancient times the catechumens were in some areas dismissed before these prayers: in other regions the dismissal took place afterwards. However, in popular speech they are often called the "General Intercessions" since they extend beyond the needs and concerns of the local community. And yet the word "intercessions" properly refers to those prayer requests included within the Eucharistic Prayer, namely, for the Church and its leaders, for reconciliation and unity, and for the salvation of all.

The Prayer of the Faithful has the following structure: 1) the celebrant addresses the people and relates the Prayer of the Faithful the mystery being celebrated, the feast, memorial or season, or to some particular aspect of the Scriptures that have been proclaimed; 2) the deacon or in his absence another minister announces a series of intentions with the people responding after each intention; 3) after a brief period of silent prayer the celebrant addresses the Father, summarizing the intentions, and asks God to look favorably upon the prayers of the congregation which, in turn, responds *Amen*.

Since the Church is both local and universal, at least one intention is usually taken from each of the following categories: 1) the needs of the Church; 2) public authorities and the salvation of the world; 3) those oppressed by any need; 4) the local community. The examples of the intentions found in the Missal are to serve as models guiding the parish community in composing intentions which are not only universal and local but also current to the changing events of the world.

Although the Prayer of the Faithful expresses and embodies in a particular way the intercessory role that belongs to all the baptized, the presentation of the intentions is especially confided to the deacon whose particular ministry was, in the early Church, focused upon the sick, the poor, widows, etc.,

Documentation

General Instruction of the Roman Missal, Third Typical Edition

69. In the Prayer of the Faithful, the people respond in a certain way to the word of God which they have welcomed in faith and, exercising the office of their baptismal priesthood, offer prayers to God for the salvation of all. It is fitting that such a prayer be included, as a rule, in Masses celebrated with a congregation, so that petitions will be offered for the holy Church, for civil authorities, for those weighed down by various needs, for all men and women, and for the salvation of the whole world.

70. As a rule, the series of intentions is to be:
    a) for the needs of the Church;
    b) for public authorities and the salvation of the whole world;
    c) for those burdened by any kind of difficulty;
    d) for the local community.
    Nevertheless, in a particular celebration, such as a confirmation, a marriage, or a funeral, the series of intentions may reflect more closely the particular occasion.

71. It is for the priest celebrant to direct this prayer from the chair. He himself begins it with a brief introduction, by which he invites the faithful to pray, and likewise he concludes it with a prayer. The intentions announced should be sober, be composed freely but prudently, and be succinct, and they should express the prayer of the entire community.
    The intentions are announced from the ambo or from another suitable place, by the deacon or by a cantor, a lector, or one of the lay faithful.
    The people, however, stand and give expression to their prayer either by an invocation said together after each intention or by praying in silence.

138. After the recitation of the Creed, the priest, standing at the chair with hands joined, by means of a brief introduction invites the faithful to participate in the Prayer of the Faithful. Then the cantor, the lector, or another person announces the intentions from the ambo or from some other suitable place while facing the people, who take their part by responding in supplication. After the intentions, the priest, with hands extended, concludes the petitions with a prayer.

43. The faithful should stand … during the Profession of Faith and the Prayer of the Faithful …

Lectionary for Mass: Introduction

30. In the light of God's word and in a sense in response to it, the congregation of the faithful prays in the universal prayer as a rule for the needs of the universal Church and the local community, for the salvation of the world and those oppressed by any burden, and for special categories of people.

The celebrant introduces the prayer; a deacon, another minister, or some of the faithful may propose intentions that are short and phrased with a measure of freedom. In these petitions "the people, exercising its priestly function, makes intercession for all men and women," with the result that, as the Liturgy of the Word has its full effects in the faithful, they are better prepared to proceed to the Liturgy of the Eucharist.

31. For the prayer of the faithful the celebrant presides at the chair and the intentions are announced at the ambo.
The assembled congregation takes part in the prayer of the faithful while standing and by saying or singing a common response after each intention or by silent prayer.

Music in Catholic Worship

74. Litanies are often more effective when sung. The repetition of melody and rhythm draws the people together in a strong and unified response. In addition to the "Lamb of God," already mentioned, the general intercessions (prayer of the faithful) offer an opportunity for litanical singing …

Reflection

The Prayer of the Faithful is an integral part of the Liturgy. Having heard the word, the assembled people respond to it, are confident that God will act today (through us) as he has in the past, and thus "exercising the office of their baptismal priesthood," they "offer prayers to God for the salvation of all" (GIRM no. 69). The entire people of God form a "royal priesthood" (1 Peter 2:9) who, in union with Christ, in solidarity with their brothers and sisters everywhere, and under the presidency of the priest, make "petitions, prayers, intercessions … for all" (1 Timothy 2:1).

Suggested Questions for Discussion

1. What is the purpose of the Prayer of the Faithful?
2. To whom is the introduction addressed? For what purpose?
3. By whom should the petitions be announced?
4. How long should each petition be?
5. Is there a tendency to lengthen unduly the number of petitions?
6. Is there a danger of excessively localizing the petitions?
7. Are the petitions ever sung? How effectively?
8. Is the nature of the petitions ever misunderstood, e.g., "For the love we experienced together …"?
9. What should be the pace and the length of the petitions?
10. Is the people's response ever sung?
11. How often should this response be varied?
12. Is it ever necessary to announce beforehand the text of the response?
13. Is silence ever used as a response to the petitions?
13. What is the nature of the concluding prayer? To whom is it addressed?
14. What are the advantages and/or disadvantages of using prepackaged announcements of the intentions?

Liturgy of the Eucharist

20
General Overview

Historical Survey

The New Testament accounts of the Last Supper highlight certain foundational actions of Jesus at the meal he shared with his Apostles on the occasion of the Passover. Toward the beginning of the meal proper he 1) took bread; 2) gave thanks; 3) broke bread; 4) and gave the bread to his disciples; toward the end of the meal Christ 5) took a cup of wine; 6) gave thanks; 7) and shared the cup with those present. The primitive Christian community, conscious of Christ's command that his followers break bread and share the cup "in memory" of him, continued these actions of Jesus and did so within a meal, at first a Jewish meal with its traditional prayers and rituals. Although it is highly probable that the Last Supper was a Passover meal, there is no evidence that the Christian celebration of the Eucharist retained the ritual form of the Passover meal, much less its occurrence only once each year.

A number of factors were soon to exert great influence upon the structure of the eucharistic celebration. First, there were certain practical difficulties in serving a regular meal every week to an increasingly large number of people. There is also evidence that certain divisive abuses at times occurred in conjunction with the common meal (see 1 Corinthians 11:18). Furthermore, once Christianity began to spread into a Gentile milieu, there was a danger that the Eucharist might be confused with meals associated with pagan mystery religions or certain political movements. As a consequence there two major changes occurred, perhaps taking place somewhat simultaneously. The Eucharist was gradually disengaged from the meal: the bread and cup rites to which Christ had attached a new meaning in reference to himself were at first celebrated either before or after the meal and eventually completely apart from the meal. And since there was an evident parallelism existing between the bread rite and the cup rite, a process of ritual simplification took place. As Dom Gregory Dix has pointed out in his monumental *Shape of the Liturgy,* the seven actions of Christ became four actions. Bread and wine were "taken" and placed on the table together; one prayer of thanksgiving to God was offered over the bread and the wine together; and finally the consecrated bread and wine were distributed. Although the precise details of this evolution are not always clear, all historically known liturgies have preserved this four-action shape of the Eucharist.

Documentation

General Instruction of the Roman Missal, Third Typical Edition

72. At the Last Supper Christ instituted the Paschal Sacrifice and banquet by which the Sacrifice of the Cross is continuously made present in the Church whenever the priest, representing Christ the Lord, carries out what the Lord himself did and handed over to his disciples to be done in his memory.

For Christ took the bread and the chalice and gave thanks; he broke the bread and gave it to his disciples, saying, "Take, eat, and drink: this is my Body; this is the cup of my Blood. Do this in memory of me." Accordingly, the Church has arranged the entire celebration of the Liturgy of the Eucharist in parts corresponding to precisely these words and actions of Christ:

1. At the Preparation of the Gifts, the bread and the wine with water are brought to the altar, the same elements that Christ took into his hands.
2. In the Eucharistic Prayer, thanks is given to God for the whole work of salvation, and the offerings become the Body and Blood of Christ.

Through the fraction and through Communion, the faithful, though they are many, receive from the one bread the Lord's Body and from the one chalice the Lord's Blood in the same way the Apostles received them from Christ's own hands.

Reflection

"At the Last Supper, on the night when He was betrayed, our Savior instituted the Eucharistic Sacrifice of His Body and Blood. He did this in order to perpetuate the Sacrifice of the Cross throughout the centuries until He should come again, and so to entrust to His beloved spouse, the Church, a memorial of His death and resurrection: a sacrament of love, a sign of unity, a bond of charity, a paschal banquet in which Christ is consumed, the mind is filled with grace, and a pledge of future glory is given to us" (Constitution on the Sacred Liturgy, art. 47). The connection between the Eucharist and the Church is so close, so intimate, that the French theologian Henri de Lubac (1896–1991) could write: "The Eucharist makes the Church, the Church makes the Eucharist."

A. Preparation of the Gifts

21
General Overview

Historical Survey

The taking of bread and wine by Christ at the Last Supper was a gesture of pointing out, of calling attention to these elements. In the early Christian community this action remained rather simple. At Rome bread and a cup of wine mixed with water were presented by the deacons to the Bishop who then began the Eucharistic Prayer. In time the Bishop said an oration over the bread and the wine before beginning this prayer. The rite seems to have expanded gradually with the people themselves bringing the gifts to the altar. In the early Middle Ages, there appeared various private prayers recited by the priest, some expressing his unworthiness, others tending to anticipate the meaning of the Eucharistic Prayer and even speaking of "offering" the gifts. As a result of these additions the rite became quite complex and was called the offertory; in some places it was known as the "Little Canon."

The Order of Mass attempts to simplify the structure of the rite by eliminating or at least modifying many of the medieval additions. To avoid possible misunderstandings it also alters the focus of the rite, which is no longer called the offertory but rather the Preparation of the Gifts. Nonetheless, a certain amount of sacrificial terminology remains.

Documentation

General Instruction of the Roman Missal, Third Typical Edition

43. They [the faithful] should, however, sit … while the Preparation of the Gifts at the Offertory is taking place …
    With a view to a uniformity in gestures and postures during one and the same celebration, the faithful should follow the directions which the deacon, lay minister, or priest gives according to whatever is indicated in the Missal.

Music in Catholic Worship

46. The eucharistic prayer is preceded by the preparation of the gifts. The purpose of the rite is to prepare bread and wine for the sacrifice. The secondary character of the rite determines the manner of the celebration. It consists very simply of bringing the gifts to the altar, possibly accompanied by song, prayers to be said by the celebrant as he prepares the gifts and the prayer over the gifts. Of these elements the bringing of the gifts, the placing of the gifts on the altar, and the prayer over the gifts are primary. All else is secondary.

Reflection

The preparation of the altar and gifts, although the beginning of the eucharistic celebration, has a secondary character since it prepares for and leads to the Eucharistic Prayer. The altar is prepared; the gifts are "set apart" and presented as a sign of the community's desire to incorporate itself in the sacrifice of Christ; the bread and the wine are placed on the altar as the celebrant praises God for his gifts which will become the body and blood of the Lord; finally, in the prayer over the gifts the priest sums up the meaning of all that has taken place. The purpose of the rite is to prepare the altar, the gifts, and the community for the offering to come. It has been called the "entering in" of the eucharistic celebration.

Suggested Questions for Discussion

1. What is the purpose of this rite?
2. Why do some still call it the "offertory"?
3. Is the meaning of the rite ever explained to the faithful?
4. What are the rite's principal elements?

22
Preparation of the Altar

Historical Survey

The manner of preparing the altar was quite simple originally. Once a linen cloth was spread upon the table, the bread and wine brought by ministers and people were placed upon it. This unpretentious action soon came to be embellished. According to a description of the papal Mass celebrated in the late seventh century, an acolyte, carrying a chalice over which was laid a large folded cloth or corporal, approached the altar. A deacon took the corporal, placed it on the right side of the altar and threw its open end to a second deacon on the other side in order to spread it over the entire top. A large chalice was then placed on the altar, and all proceeded to receive the bread and wine brought by the members of the congregation.

During the Middle Ages the spreading of the cloth occurred at various times, e.g., during the Epistle or after the Gospel. The chalice was placed on the altar before the Introit, before or after the Gospel, or after the Creed. In time the corporal and chalice were brought to the altar at the beginning of the celebration along with a purificator whose use became universally obligatory only in the sixteenth century. And yet a vestige of the older custom was retained in Solemn High Masses when the corporal, now reduced in size, was carried by the deacon to the altar during the Creed or immediately before the offertory. The chalice and purificator were usually taken to the altar at the beginning of the offertory.

Today the altar is prepared at the beginning of the preparation rite when the corporal, purificator, chalice, and Missal are placed upon it. Since this is a ministerial task, it is carried out by someone other than the presiding priest, i.e., by a deacon or acolyte.

Documentation

General Instruction of the Roman Missal, Third Edition

73. … First, the altar, the Lord's table, which is the center of the whole Liturgy of the Eucharist, is prepared by placing on it the corporal, purificator, Missal, and chalice (unless the chalice is prepared at the credence table). …

139. … An acolyte or other lay minister arranges the corporal, the purificator, the chalice, the pall, and the Missal upon the altar.

Reflection

"The Christian altar is by its very nature a table of sacrifice and at the same time a table of the paschal banquet: a unique altar on which the sacrifice of the cross is perpetuated in mystery throughout the ages until Christ comes; a table at which the Church's children assemble to give thanks to God and receive the body and blood of Christ" *(Dedication of a Church and an Altar,* Chapter IV, no. 4). Its preparation at this time makes clear that something new is beginning. Just as the ambo was the focal point of the Liturgy of the Word, so the altar-table is the focal point of the Eucharistic Liturgy.

Suggested Questions for Discussion
1. Why is the altar prepared at this time?
2. Who prepares the altar? Why?
3. Should the corporal and missal be on the altar before it is prepared for the eucharistic celebration?
4. What is the purpose of the corporal? What should be its dimensions?
5. What is the purpose of the pall? When is it needed?
6. When many communicants will receive from the chalice, where are the chalices placed so as to avoid clutter on the altar?

23
Presentation of the Gifts

Historical Survey

One of the most ancient customs of the Church is that of the people themselves providing the bread and wine for the Eucharist. In third-century Rome the deacons carried and presented to the bishop the gifts brought by the faithful. It has been suggested that by the fourth century the people processed to special tables in the transepts of Roman basilicas. The bread and wine which they placed upon these tables were then brought by the deacons to the altar. In seventh-century Rome the Pope received the bread from the aristocracy; his assistants collected bread from the others; an archdeacon received the flasks of wine. As the Roman Liturgy spread to other lands, this rite became a true procession of all the people who brought forth not only bread and wine but at times also oil, candles, wheat, grapes, and other items of precious value. Since this procession was a counterpart of the Communion procession in which the transformed bread and wine were received back, those who presented gifts were expected to receive the Eucharist.

The decrease in the number of communicants as well as the change from leavened to unleavened bread contributed to the gradual disappearance of the procession. Although traces of the procession continued down to the end of the Middle Ages, the presentation of bread and wine by the faithful was, from the eleventh century, generally replaced by the giving of money.

The Order of Mass has restored the procession in a simple form. Representative members of the assembly bring up the bread and wine together with other gifts for the poor or for the Church.

Documentation

General Instruction of the Roman Missal, Third Typical Edition

73. At the beginning of the Liturgy of the Eucharist the gifts, which will become Christ's Body and Blood, are brought to the altar.
    First, the altar, the Lord's table, which is the center of the whole Liturgy of the Eucharist, is prepared by placing on it the corporal, purificator, Missal, and chalice (unless the chalice is prepared at the credence table).
    The offerings are then brought forward. It is praiseworthy for the bread and wine to be presented by the faithful. They are then accepted at an appropriate place by the priest or the deacon and carried to the altar. Even though the faithful no longer bring from their own possessions the bread and wine intended for the liturgy as in the past, nevertheless the rite of carrying up the offerings still retains its force and its spiritual significance.

It is well also that money or other gifts for the poor or for the Church, brought by the faithful or collected in the church, should be received. These are to be put in a suitable place but away from the Eucharistic table.

140. It is appropriate for the faithful's participation to be expressed by an offering, whether of the bread and wine for the celebration of the Eucharist or of other gifts for the relief of the needs of the Church and of the poor.

The offerings of the faithful are received by the priest, assisted by the acolyte or other minister. The bread and wine for the Eucharist are carried to the celebrant, who places them upon the altar, while other gifts are put in another appropriate place …

Reflection

The procession of the gifts, which in a way parallels the Communion procession, is intended to carry on the same "force and … spiritual significance" (GIRM no. 73) of what the people did when they brought bread and wine for the liturgy from their homes. It is a symbolic expression of the gathered assembly's participation in the Eucharist and in the social mission of the Church.

Suggested Questions for Discussion

1. What is the purpose of the presentation of the gifts?
2. Where are the gifts placed before the procession?
3. What should be carried in the procession?
4. When should the procession begin?
5. Who carries the gifts and how are these persons selected?
6. What is the pace of the procession?
7. How is it organized?
8. To whom are the gifts to be presented?
9. Where are the gifts placed in the sanctuary?
10. How often is part of the collection used on behalf of the poor?
11. When should "second collections" take place?

24
Music at the Presentation/Preparation of the Gifts

Historical Survey

The practice of accompanying the presentation of the gifts with song may have originated in Africa where it was known by St. Augustine (354–430). At Rome two alternating choirs sang the psalm verses with an antiphon occurring at the beginning and end of the psalmody. Since the purpose of the singing was to accompany the procession and the reception of the gifts, the gradual loss of the procession resulted in a curtailment of the text, leaving on most occasions no more than an antiphon sung by the choir. Interestingly enough, the traditional Latin antiphons had no specifically eucharistic theme.

The *General Instruction of the Roman Missal*, although not specifying a particular purpose, suggests that singing accompany the procession until the gifts have been placed on the altar. Song, however, is not always necessary nor desirable.

Documentation

General Instruction of the Roman Missal, Third Typical Edition

74. The procession bringing the gifts is accompanied by the Offertory chant … which continues at least until the gifts have been placed on the altar. The norms on the manner of singing are the same as for the Entrance chant … Singing may always accompany the rite at the offertory, even when there is no procession with the gifts.

Music in Catholic Worship

71. The offertory song may accompany the procession and preparation of the gifts. It is not always necessary or desirable. Organ or instrumental music is also fitting at this time. When song is used, it need not speak of bread and wine or of offering. The proper function of this song is to accompany and celebrate the communal aspects of the procession. The text, therefore, can be any appropriate song of praise or of rejoicing in keeping with the season. The antiphons of the Roman Gradual, not included in the new Roman Missal, may be used with psalm verses. Instrumental interludes can effectively accompany the procession and preparation of the gifts and thus keep this part of the Mass in proper perspective relative to the eucharistic prayer which follows.

Liturgical Music Today

19. While the responsorial form of singing is especially suitable for processions, the metrical hymn can also fulfill the function of the entrance song. If, however, a metrical hymn with several verses is selected, its form should be respected. The progression of text and music must be allowed to play out its course and achieve its purpose musically and poetically. In other words, the hymn should not be ended

indiscriminately at the end of the procession. For this same reason, metrical hymns may not be the most suitable choices to accompany the preparation of the gifts and altar at the Eucharist, since the music should not extend past the time necessary for the ritual.

Reflection

The function of the song at the presentation of the gifts is to accompany the procession and highlight its communal aspects. Texts expressing praise and joy as well as seasonal texts are appropriate. The lyrics need not speak of bread and wine or of offering. To be avoided are texts that speak of offering apart from the action of Christ. Since the Preparation and Presentation of the Gifts is a secondary rite, soft instrumental music (outside Lent) or silence may be preferred as a fitting preparation for the Eucharistic Prayer.

Suggested Questions for Discussion

1. Why does the *General Instruction of the Roman Missal* refer to this song as an "offertory chant"?
2. What is its purpose?
3. What texts are appropriate?
4. By whom is it sung?
5. When does it begin? How long does it last?
6. Is song always necessary? What may suitably replace it? On what occasions?
7. What variability is possible in regard to the use of instrumental music/silence during the preparation rite?

25
Prayers at the Preparation of the Gifts

Historical Survey
Until the eleventh century the Roman Mass knew only one prayer during the preparation rite, i.e., the prayer said over the gifts immediately before the Eucharistic Prayer. But once the procession with the gifts began to disappear, various prayers were added to accompany and fill out the actions of the rite. Such texts, first appearing outside Rome, varied in different missals till they were standardized by the Missal of Pius V (1570). Designed to deepen the spirituality of the priest, they often employed sacrificial terminology and at times were even understood as anticipating the meaning of the Eucharistic Prayer.

The Order of Mass not only reduces the number of these prayers but also, to avoid possible misunderstanding, focuses on praise of God, rather than on offering. The priest raises the bread a little above the altar and prays a formula, modeled on a Jewish table prayer said by the father of the family, which blesses or praises God as the creator of the world for the gift of bread. After the cup has been prepared, the priest says a similar prayer praising the Father for the gift of wine. At the conclusion of each prayer the faithful may, if fitting, make an acclamation.

Documentation
General Instruction of the Roman Missal, Third Typical Edition

141. At the altar the priest accepts the paten with the bread. With both hands he holds it slightly raised above the altar and says quietly, *Benedictus es, Domine (Blessed are you, Lord)*. Then he places the paten with the bread on the corporal.
142. After this, as the minister presents the cruets, the priest stands at the side of the altar and pours wine and a little water into the chalice, saying quietly, *Per huius aquae (By the mystery of this water)*. He returns to the middle of the altar, takes the chalice with both hands, raises it a little, and says quietly, *Benedictus es, Domine (Blessed are you, Lord)*. Then he places the chalice on the corporal and covers it with a pall, as appropriate.

Reflection
These texts, which could be termed private prayers in the sense that they may be recited quietly by the priest, recall the source, meaning, and goal of the gifts. God is praised for the works of creation. Bread and wine, being the God-given fruits of the earth, symbolize our world, our life, and our labor. They are presented in view of what they will become, i.e., our bread of life and our spiritual drink.

Suggested Questions for Discussion

1. What is the purpose of these prayers?
2. When are they said quietly? When aloud?
3. When said aloud, what should be the manner of their recitation?
4. Why are the bread and chalice raised over the altar? Why are they only raised slightly?
5. What is the relationship between these prayers of praise and the Eucharistic Prayer?
6. Why is there a separate prayer over the bread and another over the chalice?
7. On occasions when Communion will be distributed under both species, some celebrants pour the wine to be consecrated into two chalices, one from which the celebrant receives, the other from which the people receive. What do you think about this practice?

26
Mixing of Water and Wine

Historical Survey
The mixing of water and wine is an ancient liturgical practice in both east and west. Because of the wine's heavy texture it became customary in both secular and religious usage to dilute the wine with water to render it less strong—something sober folks did. The early Christians continued this custom in the celebration of the Eucharist. This utilitarian action was soon endowed with a symbolic interpretation. In the west the mingling came to represent the union of Christ with the faithful: just as wine receives water, so Christ takes us and our sins to himself. St. Cyprian of Carthage (c. 200/210–258) in a letter against those who would use only water in the eucharistic celebration wrote: "we see that the water stands for the people whereas the wine stands for the blood of Christ. When water is united with the wine in the cup, the people are made one with Christ; the believing people are joined and united with him in whom they believe" (Letter 63). The eastern interpretation was that the wine and water represent the divine and human natures in Christ. At Rome the rite was eventually given a prayer whose text was taken from an ancient Christmas oration expressing both symbolic meanings. Today an abbreviated version of this prayer is said softly by the priest.

Documentation
General Instruction of the Roman Missal, Third Typical Edition
142. After this, as the minister presents the cruets, the priest stands at the side of the altar and pours wine and a little water into the chalice, saying quietly, *Per huius aquae (By the mystery of this water)*. He returns to the middle of the altar, takes the chalice with both hands, raises it a little, and says quietly, *Benedictus es, Domine (Blessed are you, Lord)*. Then he places the chalice on the corporal and covers it with a pall, as appropriate.

Reflection
The mixing of water and wine, seemingly maintained for reasons of tradition, recalls that what was initiated in the Incarnation is realized in the Sacrament of the Lord's Body and Blood. Through the Eucharist we are to share in the divine dignity of Christ who became incarnate for us.

Suggested Questions for Discussion
1. What is the purpose of this action?
2. What does it add to the celebration?
3. How do people understand it?

27 "Lord God, We Ask You"

Historical Survey

One of the private prayers that entered the preparation rite during the Middle Ages is the *In spiritu humilitatis*. Its text is taken from the Book of Daniel 3:39–40 where it is prayed by Azariah who, missing the sacrifices of the temple, realizes that it is the spiritual sacrifice which best pleases God. First appearing in various prayer books of the time, the text gradually became part of the preparation rite and was made obligatory with the Missal of Pius V (1570).

The prayer is retained by the Order of Mass. Being a private prayer of the priest, it is recited inaudibly.

Documentation

General Instruction of the Roman Missal, Third Typical Edition
143. After placing the chalice upon the altar, the priest bows profoundly and says quietly, *In spiritu humilitatis (Lord God, we ask you to receive us)*.

Reflection

Looking forward to the Eucharistic Prayer, the priest requests that the future offering, animated by the spiritual sacrifices of the heart, be favorably received by God.

Suggested Questions for Discussion
1. What is the purpose of this prayer?
2. What does it contribute to the Preparation of the Gifts?

28 Incensation

Historical Survey

The original Roman practice was to burn incense in a brazier which was carried in procession at the beginning and end of the celebration as well as at the Gospel. In the seventh century and perhaps under eastern influence certain northern countries introduced an incensation of the gifts on the altar. In spite of Rome's initial refusal to accept this addition, by the fourteenth century the rite was fully developed even at Rome with a blessing of the incense, an incensation of the gifts and altar with special prayers and complex gestures, and finally the incensation of the clergy and people.

Today this incensation is somewhat simplified. Bread and wine, altar, cross, priest and people are incensed in silence.

Documentation

General Instruction of the Roman Missal, Third Typical Edition

75. The bread and wine are placed on the altar by the priest to the accompaniment of the prescribed formulas. The priest may incense the gifts placed upon the altar and then incense the cross and the altar itself, so as to signify the Church's offering and prayer rising like incense in the sight of God. Next, the priest, because of his sacred ministry, and the people, by reason of their baptismal dignity, may be incensed by the deacon or another minister.

144. If incense is used, the priest then puts some in the thurible, blesses it without saying anything, and incenses the offerings, the cross, and the altar. A minister, while standing at the side of the altar, incenses the priest and then the people.

276. Thurification or incensation is an expression of reverence and prayer, as is signified in Sacred Scripture (cf. Psalm 141 [140]:2; Revelation 8:3.
    Incense may be used if desired in any form of Mass …
    d) After the bread and the chalice have been placed upon the altar, to incense the offerings, the cross, and the altar, as well as the priest and the people …

277. The priest, having put incense into the thurible, blesses it with the sign of the Cross, without saying anything.
    Before and after an incensation, a profound bow is made to the person or object that is incensed, except for the incensation of the altar and the offerings for the Sacrifice of the Mass.
    The following are incensed with three swings of the thurible: the Most Blessed Sacrament … the offerings for the sacrifice of the Mass, the altar cross … the priest, and the people.
    The altar is incensed with a series of single swings of the censer (thurible) in this way:
    a) If the altar is freestanding, the priest incenses it as he walks around it;

b) If the altar is not freestanding, the priest incenses it while walking first to the right hand side, then to the left.

The cross, if situated on or near the altar, is incensed by the priest before he incenses the altar; otherwise, he incenses it when he passes in front of it.

The priest incenses the offerings with three swings of the thurible or by making the sign of the cross over the offerings with the thurible, then going on to incense the cross and the altar.

Reflection

Incense is a traditional symbol of prayer arising to God (see Psalm 141:2; Revelation 8:3–4). Thus the gifts and altar may be incensed as a sign of the "Church's offering and prayer … rising" to God (GIRM no. 75). Priest and people are also incensed since they are to unite themselves and their prayers with the gifts which will be offered in the Eucharistic Prayer.

Suggested Questions for Discussion

1. What is the purpose of this incensation?
2. Does it duplicate the incensation at the beginning of the celebration?
3. On what occasions is it especially appropriate?
4. In what manner are the gifts on the altar incensed?
5. What sign of veneration is required while passing in front of the altar?
6. What is the posture of the people during their incensation?

29
Washing of Hands

Historical Survey

Washing one's hands as a sign of inner purity was customary in both Judaism and early Christianity. The Roman Mass has historically known various washings of the hands, sometimes before the gifts of the people were collected, sometimes afterwards. It has been suggested that the original purpose of the gesture within the liturgy was not for purposes of physical cleanliness but as a symbol of the interior purity required before entering into the sacred mystery. At any rate, a hand washing at this place first appeared outside Rome, and it survived only in a Mass presided over by a priest. At first no prayer accompanied the action, but a number of formulas were added as early as the eleventh century. The most general of these was one or more verses of Psalm 26. In the sixteenth century Psalm 26:6–12 and a concluding doxology were made obligatory.

Today the washing of the hands is accompanied by Psalm 51:2, which is said quietly by the priest.

Documentation

General Instruction of the Roman Missal, Third Typical Edition

76. The priest then washes his hands at the side of the altar, a rite that is an expression of his desire for interior purification.
145. After the prayer *In spiritu humilitatis (Lord God, we ask you to receive us)* or after the incensation, the priest washes his hands standing at the side of the altar and, as the minister pours the water, says quietly, *Lava me, Domine (Lord, wash away my iniquity)*.

Reflection

The washing of the hands is a symbolic and private action expressing the celebrant's need for inward purification.

Suggested Questions for Discussion

1. What is the purpose of the washing of the hands?
2. How does it serve the assembly?
3. What is its relationship to other penitential actions in the celebration?
4. What is the size and quality of the towel and basin?
5. Why are the hands of the minister and not his fingers washed?

30
Prayer over the Offerings and Its Invitation

Historical Survey

In the ancient Roman Liturgy, once the bread and wine were placed on the altar, the Bishop said a prayer over these gifts and then began the Eucharistic Prayer. By the eighth century and in Frankish countries a short invitation to pray, followed by silence, was introduced before the prayer over the gifts. Sometimes the invitation was addressed quietly to the assisting clergy, sometimes aloud to the whole assembly. Since the celebrant was requesting silent prayer, no formulated response was required. Gradually, however, a variety of spoken responses replaced the time for prayerful silence. The present formula came into general use after the eleventh century. Today the priest addresses the invitation to the whole congregation which prays that the sacrifice will be acceptable and pleasing to the Father.

The Prayer over the Offerings was originally said aloud. The first evidence for its silent recitation comes from eighth century Frankish territory. This custom, perhaps due to eastern influence, gradually became more widespread. Whereas in Rome the formula was long known as the "Prayer over the Offerings," the Frankish designation was the "secret," most probably reflecting the silent manner of saying the prayer whose conclusion alone was said aloud or sung by the priest. Another explanation for the designation might be that the prayer was said over the offerings that had been "set aside."

The Order of Mass restores the prayer's original name and manner of recitation. Its invitation is addressed to the people who are standing (this posture being introduced by the Third Edition of the *General Instruction*).

Documentation

General Instruction of the Roman Missal, Third Typical Edition

77. Once the offerings have been placed on the altar and the accompanying rites completed, the invitation to pray with the priest and the prayer over the offerings conclude the preparation of the gifts and prepare for the Eucharistic Prayer.
    In the Mass, only one Prayer over the Offerings is said, and it ends with the shorter conclusion: Per *Christum Dominum nostrum*. If, however, the Son is mentioned at the end of this prayer, the conclusion is, *Qui vivit et regnat in saecula saeculorum*. The people, uniting themselves to this entreaty, make the prayer their own with the acclamation, *Amen*.

146. Upon returning to the middle of the altar, the priest, facing the people and extending and then joining his hands, invites the people to pray, saying, *Orate, fraters (Pray, brethren)*. The people rise and make their response: *Suscipiat Dominus*

(May the Lord accept). Then the priest, with hands extended, says the prayer over the offerings. At the end the people make the acclamation, *Amen*.
43. The faithful should stand … from the invitation, *Orate, fratres (Pray, brethren)*, before the prayer over the offerings until the end of Mass, except at the places indicated below …

Reflection

The prayer over the offerings concludes the preparation of the bread, wine, altar, and community. Its invitation, which like similar introductions may be creatively adapted to circumstances and occasions, serves as the introduction to the prayer and articulates the sacrificial character of the Mass. The people's response indicates the congregation's link with the priest and also distinguishes a certain duality of aspects in the Liturgy: the worship of God and the sanctification of the faithful. Whereas the Collect is more expansive and frequently characterizes the mystery of the day or liturgical season, the prayer over the offerings is more concise. It requests divine acceptance and expresses the community's desire to unite itself with the offering to come.

Suggested Questions for Discussion

1. Why do the people stand for this prayer and its introduction?
2. What is the purpose of the initial invitation?
3. What gesture accompanies this invitation? What is its purpose?
4. In what manner should the invitation be given?
5. What is the purpose of the people's response? Do the people find it easy to recite?
6. Upon whom or what should the celebrant focus his attention during this response?
7. What is the purpose of the prayer over the offerings?
8. How does it differ from the short prayers of praise said earlier over the offerings?
9. What gesture is used by the priest as he says the prayer over the offerings? What is the meaning of this gesture?

B. Eucharistic Prayer

31
General Overview

Historical Survey

Recent decades have seen much scholarly research, and from a number of perspectives, into the origins of the Eucharistic Prayer which in Latin was traditionally called the *canon* (from the Latin/Greek for "rule" or "law") and in the east as the *anaphora* (from the Greek for "elevation" or "uplifting"). There is almost universal agreement that the beginnings of the Eucharistic Prayer are closely connected with a series of table prayers required at every Jewish meal. These assumed the greatest importance on such holy days as the feast of the Passover. Toward the beginning of the meal the father of the family or the presiding member of the community uttered a Jewish prayer of blessing, known in Hebrew as a *berakah,* which blessed or praised God. Holding the bread the one presiding prayed: "Blessed are you, Lord, our God, king of the world, who has brought bread from heaven." The bread was then broken and distributed to those present. The various courses of the meal followed, with the Passover meal being distinguished by special foods, prayers, and the recitation of the *haggadah.* The latter interpreted the special meaning of the feast as one which made present God's liberating deeds of the past and applied their power to those celebrating the feast.

Toward the end of the meal and over a cup of wine the presider said another though more solemn and extensive *berakah* which, after an initial dialogue, consisted of three sections. The first praised God for all creation, especially the creation of life. The second was a thanksgiving for the whole history of salvation, i.e., for a desirable and ample land, for the covenant, for the law. The third section was a supplication that God's creative and redemptive action be continued and renewed, especially in the coming of the Messiah and in the restoration of the house of David. On certain festive occasions this section was expanded by a request that God accept the "remembrance" of his people, namely, that God, ever faithful to his covenant, might continue to renew his great deeds.

Whether the Last Supper was an actual Passover meal has long been debated. The Synoptics indicate it was: the Johannine Gospel implies it was not. Various attempts have been made to reconcile the two accounts. At any rate, the Last Supper had strong Passover connotations for the early Christians. But what is especially significant is that Jesus, while using the traditional meal *berakoth,* gave them a new dimension with his words "This is my Body" and "This is my Blood." The memorial interpolation within the third section of the prayer over the cup might have been the occasion for Christ to explain his command "Do this in memory of me."

The Apostles continued to gather for table fellowship after Christ's Resurrection and Ascension. When they gathered to break bread, they did so "in memory" of the Lord. The traditional Jewish prayer forms over the bread and cup were used, although they were understood and perhaps somewhat altered in light of the primitive community's experience of the Lord. But already in apostolic times a process of simplification and unification occurred, perhaps in conjunction with the separation of the Eucharist from the regular meal.

Since the prayer over the bread was so brief, the more lengthy and theologically developed blessing over the cup was used as the basis for a prayer of praise and thanksgiving said over the bread and the wine together. It is from this prototype that the Eucharistic Prayer evolved. There were no liturgical books: the presiding minister merely improvised over the *berakah's* structure with its themes of praise, thanksgiving, and supplication. A more explicit Christological coloring and expansion were eventually given these motifs, and secondary elements were added or elaborated at different points in the common basic structure. It was only in the fourth century that extemporization gave way to fixed forms which differed according to geographic regions.

Unlike the eastern liturgies where there was great creativity in developing numerous texts, the Roman rite for centuries knew only one Eucharistic Prayer, the Roman Canon. Although its Preface was variable, the rest of the Canon was fixed with, at most, some minor additions on certain days. Most probably written in Latin, its text goes back to the fourth century. The prayer underwent various elaborations till stabilized and edited by Pope Gregory the Great (590–604). The Canon was originally declaimed or sung so that it could be heard by all. But by the second half of the ninth century it came to be prayed in a low voice. This development was probably the result of the Mass being understood as a "mystery" with the priest alone entering into the "holy of holies" at this point. It was only in the 1960s that liturgical reforms allowed and even encouraged the presiding priest to say aloud the whole Eucharistic Prayer; just as The Second Vatican Council opened the Scriptures to the people, so the Eucharistic Prayer was now likewise opened.

In 1964 the *Consilium*, the official commission established at Rome to implement the liturgical decisions of Vatican II, appointed a special committee to study the Eucharistic Prayer. The Roman Canon, in spite of its venerable age and traditional witness to eucharistic doctrine in the west, evidenced certain weaknesses, e.g., its length, its numerous repetitions, its lack of structural cohesiveness, its lack of an explicit invocation of Holy Spirit, and the relative absence of elements of praise. Various reform projects were proposed, but it was soon realized that there could be no substantial modifications of the Canon without great damage to the prayer itself. Consequently it was decided to retain the Canon without major modifications and to issue alternative Eucharistic Prayer to be used along with it. In 1968 a slightly revised version of the Canon, now known as Eucharistic Prayer I, was published together with three other prayers designated as Eucharistic Prayer, II, III, and IV.

Eucharistic Prayer II, which is extremely brief and simple, is based on a model given in the *Apostolic Tradition* (c.215) usually attributed to Hippolytus of Rome. There has been a reorganization of the original material, the addition of a *Sanctus* and intercessions, a modification of the doxology, as well as a clarification or elimination of certain expressions found in the original text. A proper Preface is given, although others may be substituted, preferably from among those that speak in general terms of the whole mystery of salvation. Eucharistic Prayer III, a new composition with parts clearly arranged, incorporates the general themes of the Roman Canon and enriches them with formulas from other liturgical traditions. Prayer IV draws its substance from eastern sources (especially the Anaphora of St. Basil) and, following their example, continues the theme of praise after the *Sanctus*. For this reason its proper Preface is always used with it.

In 1974 three Eucharistic Prayers for Masses with children were approved for trial use. All are characterized by the use of acclamations. Of significant interest is that the memorial acclamations are more logically linked to the priest's prayer expressing memory and offering. There are also two Eucharistic Prayers for Reconciliation, originally intended for use during the 1975 Holy Year, which may now be used when reconciliation is a special theme of the celebration. In 1995 a Eucharistic Prayer for Masses for Various Needs and Occasions (formerly known as the Swiss Synod Eucharistic Prayer) was authorized.

Although the Eucharistic Prayer is essentially one, several elements or focal points are found in the new compositions. These structural parts, which make explicit the themes permeating the whole prayer, are listed by the *General Instruction of the Roman Missal* (no. 79) as:

1. thanksgiving;
2. acclamation;
3. epiclesis;
4. institution narrative and consecration;
5. anamnesis;
6. offering;
7. intercessions;
8. final doxology.

Documentation

General Instruction of the Roman Missal, Third Typical Edition

78. Now the center and summit of the entire celebration begins: namely, the Eucharistic Prayer, that is, the prayer of thanksgiving and sanctification. The priest invites the people to lift up their hearts to the Lord in prayer and thanksgiving; he unites the congregation with himself in the prayer that he addresses in the name of the entire community to God the Father through Jesus Christ in the Holy Spirit. Furthermore, the meaning of the Prayer is that the entire congregation of the faithful should join itself with Christ in confessing the great deeds of God and in the offering of Sacrifice. The Eucharistic Prayer demands that all listen to it with reverence and in silence.

30. Among the parts assigned to the priest, the foremost is the Eucharistic Prayer, which is the high point of the entire celebration. Next are the orations: that is to say, the collect, the prayer over the offerings, and the prayer after Communion. These prayers are addressed to God in the name of the entire holy people and all present, by the priest who presides over the assembly in the person of Christ. It is with good reason, therefore, that they are called the "presidential prayers."

31. It is also up to the priest, in the exercise of his office of presiding over the gathered assembly, to offer certain explanations that are foreseen in the rite itself. Where it is indicated in the rubrics, the celebrant is permitted to adapt them somewhat in order that they respond to the understanding of those participating. However, he should always take care to keep to the sense of the text given in the Missal and to express them succinctly. The presiding priest is also to direct the word of God and to impart the final blessing. In addition, he may give the faithful a very brief introduction to the Mass of the day (after the initial Greeting and before the Act of Penitence), to the Liturgy of the Word (before the readings), and to the Eucharistic Prayer (before the Preface), though never during the Eucharistic Prayer itself; he may also make concluding comments to the entire sacred action before the dismissal.

32. The nature of the "presidential" texts demands that they be spoken in a loud and clear voice and that everyone listen with attention. Thus, while the priest is speaking these texts, there should be no other prayers or singing, and the organ or other musical instruments should be silent.

43. … In the dioceses of the United States of America, they should kneel beginning after the singing or recitation of the *Sanctus* until after the *Amen* of the Eucharistic Prayer, except when prevented on occasion by reasons of health, lack of space, the large number of people present, or some other good reason. Those who do not kneel ought to make a profound bow when the priest genuflects after the consecration. The faithful kneel after the *Agnus Dei* unless the Diocesan Bishop determines otherwise.

    With a view to a uniformity in gestures and postures during one and the same celebration, the faithful should follow the directions which the deacon, lay minister, or priest gives according to whatever is indicated in the Missal.

147. … It is very appropriate that the priest sing those parts of the Eucharistic Prayer for which musical notation is provided.

Music in Catholic Worship

47. The eucharistic prayer, a prayer of thanksgiving and sanctification, is the center of the entire celebration. By an introductory dialogue the priest invites the people to lift their hearts to God in praise and thanks; he unites them with himself in the prayer he addresses in their name to the Father through Jesus Christ. The meaning of the prayer is that the whole congregation joins itself to Christ in acknowledging the works of God and in offering the sacrifice (GIRM 54 [78]). As a statement of the faith of the local assembly it is affirmed and ratified by all those present through acclamations of faith: the first acclamation or Sanctus, the memorial acclamation, and the Great Amen.

Liturgical Music Today

15. … it needs to be recognized that a certain musical integrity within a liturgical prayer or rite can be achieved only by unity in the musical composition. Thus, it is recommended that for the acclamations in the eucharistic prayer one musical style be employed.

17. The acclamations (... eucharistic acclamations—including the special acclamations of praise in the *Eucharistic Prayers of Masses with Children* [*Eucharistic Prayers for Masses with Children and for Masses of Reconciliation,* Provisional Text {Washington: USCC, 1975}]) are the preeminent sung prayers of the eucharistic liturgy. Singing these acclamations makes their prayer all the more effective. They should, therefore, be sung, even at weekday celebrations of the Eucharist.

Reflection

The Eucharistic Prayer, as "the center and summit of the entire celebration" (GIRM no. 78), is a summary of what it means for the Church to celebrate the Eucharist. It is essentially a statement of praise and thanksgiving, a proclamation of wonder, for God's works of salvation as well as an action that makes the Eucharist, rendering present both the Body and Blood of the Lord and the Lord's great redeeming actions. It is solemn liturgical speech par excellence. In language which is formal, poetic, and biblical the priest, addressing the Father in the name of Christ, speaks to and on behalf of the whole assembly which professes its faith and manifests its participation by joining in the initial dialogue and the acclamations.

Suggested Questions for Discussion

1. What is the meaning of the Eucharistic Prayer?
2. Do people generally understand this prayer as "the center and summit of the entire celebration" (GIRM no. 78)?
3. In what way does the whole liturgical assembly join Christ "in confessing the great things God has done and in offering the sacrifice" (ibid.)?
4. Do people experience the Eucharistic Prayer as indeed a prayer prayed in their name and not simply as a long monologue prayer by the priest?
5. What is the role of the priest in the Eucharistic Prayer?
6. On what occasions may the Eucharistic Prayers for Reconciliation be used?
7. When may the Eucharistic Prayers for Masses with Children be used?
8. How often does the priest briefly introduce the Eucharistic Prayer?
9. Is this introduction helpful?
10. Why does the congregation stand during the Preface but kneel throughout the remainder of the prayer?
11. Should the Eucharistic Prayer be sung? If so, on what occasions?
12. Is it appropriate to punctuate the whole Eucharistic Prayer with acclamations?

32
Preface

Historical Survey

Although praise and thanksgiving characterize the whole Eucharistic Prayer, these elements particularly appear in the Preface, a term meaning "proclamation" or "speaking out" before or in the presence of God and God's people.

The Preface begins with an initial dialogue whose presence—although with some variations—in all traditional Eucharistic Prayers attests its antiquity and importance. The Roman Liturgy begins with *Dominus vobiscum (The Lord be with you)* and its accustomed response, followed by the *Sursum corda (Lift up your hearts)*, a phrase found in Lamentations 3:41. The *Gratias agamus Domino Deo nostro (Let us give thanks to the Lord, our God)* was probably borrowed from Judaism where it occurred as an invitation to the prayer of blessing over the cup. Its response *Dignum et iustum est (It is right to give him thanks and praise)* is of Greek origin as an acclamation of agreement.

The body of the Preface is a statement of the special reason for praising God, especially God's work in creation and redemption. In the east the text of the Preface, presenting a rather long and general view of the whole history of salvation, is a fixed part of the Eucharistic Prayer. The type that predominated in the west was variable and stressed from day to day one particular aspect of God's saving work. The Roman Canon, for example, was at first used with a wide variety of Prefaces appointed for particular days and seasons. Gradually this number was greatly reduced.

The Missal now contains over eighty individual Prefaces for feast days, liturgical seasons, votive Masses, and special occasions. All are concise statements of praise addressed to the Father through the Son. A proper Preface is provided for Eucharistic Prayer II, although another may be substituted. Since the thematic development begun by the Preface continues beyond the *Sanctus* in Prayer IV, the Preface assigned to this prayer must always be used with it.

Documentation

General Instruction of the Roman Missal, Third Typical Edition

79a. *Thanksgiving* (expressed especially in the Preface): In which the priest, in the name of the entire holy people, glorifies God the Father and gives thanks for the whole work of salvation or for some special aspect of it that corresponds to the day, festivity, or season.

147. Then the priest begins the Eucharistic Prayer. In accordance with the rubrics (cf. below, no. 365), he selects a Eucharistic Prayer from those found in the Roman Missal or approved by the Apostolic See. The Eucharistic Prayer demands, by its very nature, that only the priest say it in virtue of his ordination. The people, for their part, should associate themselves with the priest in faith and in silence, as well as through their parts as prescribed in the course of the Eucharistic Prayer: namely

the responses in the Preface dialogue, the *Sanctus*, the acclamation after the consecration, the acclamatory *Amen* after the final doxology, as well as other acclamations approved by the Conference of Bishops and recognized by the Holy See.

It is very appropriate that the priest sing those parts of the Eucharistic Prayer for which musical notation is provided.

148. As he begins the Eucharistic Prayer, the priest extends his hands and sings or says, *Dominus vobiscum (The Lord be with you)*. The people respond, *Et cum spiritu tuo (And also with you)*. As he continues, *Sursum corda (Lift up your hearts)*, he raises his hands. The people respond, *Habemus ad Dominum (We lift them up to the Lord)*. Then the priest, with hands outstretched, adds, *Gratias agamus Domino Deo nostro (Let us give thanks to the Lord, our God)*, and the people respond, *Dignum et iustum est (It is right to give him thanks and praise)*. Next, the priest, with hands extended, continues the Preface. At its conclusion, he joins his hands, and together with everyone present, sings or says aloud the *Sanctus* (cf. above, no. 79b).

Reflection

In this solemn beginning of the Eucharistic Prayer the whole congregation through the priest blesses or praises God for his wonderful works of creation and redemption. Focusing attention on a particular mystery or aspect of salvation history or giving a quick glance at some mystery or feast being celebrated, the Preface is the keynote for the praise and thanksgiving that permeate the whole Eucharistic Prayer. In the introductory dialogue the congregation is made conscious of its close union with the presiding priest who speaks in the name of all. This dialogue parallels the *Amen* at the conclusion of the prayer: both manifest the ecclesial unity of all who praise the Father through the Son.

Suggested Questions for Discussion

1. What is the meaning of the Preface?
2. How do people understand its function in relation to the whole Eucharistic Prayer?
3. How do people understand the word "Preface"?
4. What time element separates the beginning of the Preface from the *Amen* at the conclusion of the Prayer over the Offerings?
5. On what occasions should the Preface be sung?

33
"Holy, Holy, Holy Lord"

Historical Survey

The "Holy, holy, holy Lord," a text inspired by the vision of Isaiah 6:2–3, was sung in the synagogue morning office from at least the second century. It was in the east that it made its way into the Eucharistic Prayer, perhaps through the influence of Jewish-Christians. By the mid-fifth century its incorporation in the prayer was generally accepted in the west. Even though this chant somewhat interrupts the flow of ideas, it finds a logical link in the evocation of the multitudes of angels and the seraphim which has from ancient times concluded the Preface.

The verse "Blessed is he" is the acclamation used by the people to greet Christ at his solemn entrance into Jerusalem (see Matthew 21:9). By the mid-sixth century this acclamation was already joined to the *Sanctus* in Gaul, and a century later, in Rome also.

Although the *Sanctus* was originally sung by the whole congregation, by the early Middle Ages the singing was assigned to the choir. Eventually the priest continued on with the Eucharistic Prayer during the singing. The development of complex melodies resulted in the *Benedictus* being sung after the words of institution.

Today the *Sanctus* and *Benedictus* are again joined as an acclamation sung or said by priest and people as a conclusion to the Preface.

Documentation

General Instruction of the Roman Missal, Third Typical Edition
79b. *Acclamation*: In which the whole congregation, joining with the heavenly powers, sings the Sanctus. This acclamation, which is part of the Eucharistic Prayer itself, is sung or said by all the people with the priest.

Music in Catholic Worship
56. This is the people's acclamation of praise concluding the preface of the eucharistic prayer. We join the whole communion of saints in acclaiming the Lord. Settings which add harmony or descants on solemn feasts and occasions are appropriate, but since this chant belongs to priest and people the choir parts must facilitate and make effective the people's parts.

Reflection

In this acclamation the assembly responds to the celebrant's invitation to join all creation in giving praise to the Father through Christ. With one voice the whole communion of saints gives glory to God.

Suggested Questions for Discussion
1. What is the purpose of the *Sanctus?*
2. Does it interrupt the thematic development of the Eucharistic Prayer?
3. How often is it sung? By whom?
4. Do people enjoy singing it?
5. When the *Sanctus* is sung, what time element separates it from the conclusion of the Preface?

34 Epiclesis

Historical Survey

The final section of the Jewish table prayer over the cup contains a petition, looking forward to the future, which requests the re-establishment of the house of David. Such a request would have made it quite natural for the early Christians, among whom eschatological hope was very strong, to mention the Holy Spirit, the bond of unity, toward the conclusion of the Eucharistic Prayer. At any rate, there soon developed at this point a formal petition that the Spirit come upon the community and/or upon the bread and wine. Such an invocation is technically known as an *epiclesis*, i.e., a "calling upon," a "calling over here," an "invocation." Here the Father is requested to send the Holy Spirit who brings about such fruits of the Eucharist as unity and love among the faithful. In certain eastern liturgies it is a request that the Spirit actually bless, sanctify, and transform the bread and the wine.

Another form of the epiclesis, occurring before the words of institution, requests that God accept the sacrifice, that it be filled with the blessing of the Holy Spirit. This preliminary epiclesis flows from the theme of fullness found in the *Sanctus*, namely, that heaven and earth are full of God's glory.

The Roman Canon has the equivalent of an epiclesis in the request that the Father "accept and bless these gifts" and that they become "an offering in spirit and in truth … the body and blood of Jesus Christ." After the words of institution there is also a petition that the sacrifice be borne to the heavenly altar by the hand of the Angel and that those participating in the Eucharist "be filled with every grace and blessing." In neither case, however, is there an explicit mention of the Holy Spirit.

To compensate for this lack, the new Eucharistic Prayers contain an explicit epiclesis requesting the Spirit to come. It follows a split pattern. Although in the eastern liturgies the invocation requesting the Spirit to transform the gifts appears after the institution narrative, the new prayers make this request before the narrative. It is a petition that the Father send the Holy Spirit to "make holy" (II, III) or "sanctify" (IV) the gifts so that they may become the Body and Blood of the Lord. As the priest makes this petition, he extends his hands over the bread and wine in the ancient gesture signifying the giving of the Spirit. Following the institution narrative, the acclamation, and the memorial–offering, the priest again explicitly invokes the Spirit and asks that all "be brought together in unity" (II), "become one body, one spirit in Christ" (III), and that "all who share this bread and wine" be gathered "into the one body of Christ, a living sacrifice of praise" (IV).

For centuries the Eucharistic Prayer was considered as a unified whole, and the Church was not overly concerned with the exact point at which the transformation of the bread and wine took place. And yet two theological traditions developed. Theologians in the west, starting with St. Ambrose (340–397), stressed the importance of the words of institution. The Greeks, reacting to certain heretical tendencies that attacked the divinity of the Third Person of the Trinity, placed emphasis on the action of the Holy Spirit as sanctifying both the gifts and the people. For a long time these different approaches caused no difficulties, not even in the ninth and eleventh centuries when there were disputes between the east and the west. It was only during the Middle Ages that problems arose as theologians attempted to pinpoint when and how the consecration occurred. The two understandings then became a point of bitter controversy between east and west. Recent theological reflection, however, calls attention to the dynamic and unified character of the Eucharistic Prayer.

Documentation

General Instruction of the Roman Missal, Third Typical Edition

79c. *Epiclesis*: In which, by means of particular invocations, the Church implores the power of the Holy Spirit that the gifts offered by human hands be consecrated, that is, become Christ's Body and Blood, and that the spotless Victim to be received in Communion be for the salvation of those who will partake of it.

Reflection

To sanctify is a role properly attributed to the Holy Spirit who completes and brings to fullness the work of the Father and the Son. Although the prayer for the consecration is addressed to the Father, it is through the power of the Spirit, who integrates the gifts of the people into the offering of Christ, that the Church presents to the Father the memorial of the Son and efficaciously repeats the words of institution. It is also through the Holy Spirit that the Church constantly becomes the body of Christ, nourished and fortified by his presence in the Eucharist. Both gifts and people are transformed by the power of the Spirit: the gifts of bread and wine become the signs of Christ's sacramental presence as food; the people enter into communion with Christ and with each other; they are unified, given life and sanctification. In other words, just as bread and wine are transformed into the body and blood of Christ, so by sharing the loaf and the chalice we also are to be transformed, we are to become the body of Christ, paradoxically something we already are through Baptism.

Suggested Questions for Discussion

1. What activity of the Holy Spirit is expressed by the epiclesis?
2. In what way is the epiclesis a reminder that the faithful are an assembly at prayer?
3. What is the meaning of the imposition of hands during the first epiclesis?
4. How is this gesture made?

35
Narrative of the Institution

Historical Survey

The words of institution and "consecration" are essential to the Eucharistic Prayer. Their ancient liturgical usage is already reflected in the scriptural accounts of the Last Supper which, as scholars point out, represent various traditions (e.g., Paul and Luke that of Antioch) and borrow the phrasing of these words from actual eucharistic celebrations of the apostolic Church. In the more than eighty liturgical versions of the institution narrative found in traditional Eucharistic Prayers, there are numerous differences. Although all show a concern for scriptural tradition, no attempt is made to strive for literal exactitude—liturgical tradition thus being different from scriptural tradition. The narrative is always inserted in a prayer. There is also a tendency to establish a certain parallelism between the words over the bread and those over the chalice and also to embellish the scriptural texts (giving details either not found in the scriptural institution accounts or borrowed from elsewhere in Scripture, e.g., "looking up to heaven"). The Roman Canon, for example, speaks of Jesus taking the bread and the chalice "into his holy and venerable hands" and long incorporated the phrase "mystery of faith" into the words over the chalice.

The elevation of the host at the institution narratives dates from the early thirteenth century, a time when the faithful communicated but rarely and consequently took great satisfaction in seeing the consecrated bread.

The elevation of the chalice as well as a genuflection after the consecration of the bread and another after the consecration of the wine appeared in the late fourteenth century. They gained universal acceptance with the Missal of Pius V in 1570.

All present Roman Eucharistic Prayers have the same words of institution (a uniformity requested by Pope Paul VI), although the narratives in which they are framed differ in each case. The "mystery of faith" phrase has been removed from the words over the cup and now serves to introduce the memorial acclamation, whereas the sacrificial phrase "which will be given up for you," borrowed from Luke 22:19 and 1 Corinthians 11:24, has been added to the words over the bread. The phrase "Do this in memory of me" replaces "As often as you do these things, you do them in memory of me." The elevations and genuflections remain unchanged.

Documentation

General Instruction of the Roman Missal, Third Typical Edition

79d. *Institution narrative and consecration*: In which, by means of words and actions of Christ, the Sacrifice is carried out which Christ himself instituted at the Last Supper, when he offered his Body and Blood under the species of bread and wine, gave them to his Apostles to eat and drink, and left them the command to perpetuate this same mystery.

150. A little before the consecration, when appropriate, a server rings a bell as a signal to the faithful. According to local custom, the server also rings the bell as the priest shows the host and then the chalice.
If incense is used, a server incenses the host and the chalice when each is shown to the people after the consecration.
276. Thurification or incensation is an expression of reverence and of prayer, as is signified in Sacred Scripture (cf. Ps 141 [140]:2, Rev 8:3).
Incense may be used if desired in any form of Mass ...
e) At the showing of the host and the chalice after the consecration.

Reflection

Just as the Eucharistic Prayer is part of a continuous action extending from the preparation of the gifts to the Communion, so the words of institution are part of the Eucharistic Prayer which is a consecratory, thanksgiving prayer of praise. All that God has accomplished in creation and salvation history is fulfilled, signified, and made present in the person of the crucified and risen Christ. Christ's words are a promise, and through the power of the Holy Spirit they accomplish what they signify: his eucharistic Body and Blood, his Real Presence with all the riches of the Kingdom.

Suggested Questions for Discussion

1. What is the purpose of the institution narrative?
2. How do people understand it?
3. When does the congregation do what Jesus did at the Last Supper?
4. Why is it inappropriate for the priest to break the bread as he says "broke it ..."?
5. What is the purpose of the elevations?
6. When might it be appropriate to ring the bell before the institution narrative and during the two elevations?

36
Memorial Acclamation

Historical Survey

An acclamation of the people following the words of institution is an innovation in the Roman Liturgy. And yet an analogous custom is found in certain eastern Eucharistic Prayers where the people sing *Amen* after each formula of institution.

The priest gives an invitation: *Let us proclaim the mystery of faith*. The phrase "mystery of faith," already found in a treatise on baptism written by a third-century anonymous author (called Pseudo-Cyprian), is a very ancient interpolation in various Eucharistic Prayers, appears in the oldest manuscripts of the Roman Canon where it is inserted within Christ's words over the chalice. The precise meaning of the phrase was long the subject of much discussion. Now transferred from the words of institution to the invitation calling forth the people's acclamation, its meaning is clarified by the response of the congregation. The mystery of faith is the Paschal Mystery, the mystery of Christ dying, rising, and present among his people. It is the whole plan of God realized in Christ's saving love.

Whereas the Latin gives only three acclamatory formulas, the English version presents two translations of the first Latin acclamation. With the exception of the first, all four English options remain faithful to the Latin by being addressed to Christ. Options one and two are based on a formula borrowed from the Syrian rite and recall the death, resurrection and second coming of Christ. The third option almost word for word echoes 1 Corinthians 11:26. Option four is the only acclamation that does not mention the final coming of Christ.

Documentation

General Instruction of the Roman Missal, Third Typical Edition
151. After the consecration when the priest has said, *Mysterium fidei (Let us proclaim the mystery of faith)*, the people sing or say an acclamation using one of the prescribed formulas.

Music in Catholic Worship
57. We support one another's faith in the paschal mystery, the central mystery of our belief. This acclamation is properly a memorial of the Lord's suffering and glorification, with an expression of faith in his coming. Variety in text and music is desirable.

Reflection

The memorial acclamation not only helps sustain the assembly's attention from the end of the *Sanctus* to the Great Amen, but is also a manifestation of the congregation's active participation in the Eucharistic Prayer. Sharing in the Eucharist by virtue of their baptismal priesthood, the faithful express and affirm belief that the whole mystery of the Risen Christ is present and active in the celebration.

Suggested Questions for Discussion
1. What is the purpose of the memorial acclamation?
2. Does the content of this acclamation duplicate that of the following section of the Eucharistic Prayer?
3. Is it appropriate for the minister to point to the consecrated elements as he invites all to "proclaim the mystery of faith"?
4. How are people made aware of which acclamation is to be used?
5. May memorial acclamations other than those in the Missal be used?
6. What is the nature of an acclamation? How does it differ, e.g., from an exhortation?
7. When the acclamation is sung, how soon does it follow the invitation?
8. How is the acclamation introduced musically?

37
Anamnesis

Historical Survey

The Passover is a feast whose participants make "memory" *(zikkaron* in Hebrew, *anamnesis* in Greek) of the whole saving and liberating action of God in the historical past. Yet this is not a "remembering" in our customary understanding of the word today. It is a making present, a re-actualizing for "today" of something that occurred in the past. Since God is ever faithful to his covenant, his past deeds become present and accomplish their effects for all who share in the Passover meal. It is in the context of this religious psychology that Christ uttered his command "Do this in memory of me."

The whole eucharistic action and especially the words of institution are a memorial, an actual making present of God's saving deeds in Christ so that their fullness and power take effect here and now. And yet the Church from earliest times has drawn out the implications of Christ's command by a special statement called the *anamnesis* which clearly expresses the meaning of the eucharistic memorial. This statement is closely linked to the institution narrative and normally leads to a statement of offering: "Remembering … we offer …. " Although the precise wording may vary, most traditional Eucharistic Prayers state that the Church makes memory of the Lord's passion, resurrection, and ascension. At times other aspects of the mystery of salvation are added: Christ's incarnation, burial, ascension, and future coming in glory.

The Roman Canon names the passion, resurrection, and ascension. The new Eucharistic Prayers are generally more inclusive by recalling Christ's death (II, III, IV), his descent among the dead (IV), his resurrection (II, III, IV), his ascension (III, IV), and his coming again in glory (III, IV).

Documentation

General Instruction of the Roman Missal, Third Typical Edition
79e. *Anamnesis*: In which the Church, fulfilling the command that she received from Christ the Lord through the Apostles, keeps the memorial of Christ, recalling especially his blessed Passion, glorious Resurrection, and Ascension into heaven.

Reflection

By doing what Jesus has done the Church makes living memory of Christ's saving deeds. The fullness and power of the Paschal Mystery continue to be present as an ongoing reality when the Church celebrates the Eucharist. Since the Eucharist is also the pledge of future glory, Christ's coming at the end of time is also anticipated.

Suggested Questions for Discussion
1. What is the meaning of the anamnesis?
2. Does it differ from the assembly's memorial acclamation after the institution narrative?
3. How do people understand the Eucharist as a "memorial"? As a memorial of Christ's saving deeds? As a promise of his future coming?

38 Offering

Historical Survey

Characteristic of all Eucharistic Prayers is a statement of offering. Most frequently this is linked to the anamnesis and is an explicit declaration that the Church is offering the "bread and the cup" or some other elaborated equivalent.

Emphasis on offering and the acceptance of the gifts is a theme that occurs throughout the Roman Canon. While great value is thus attributed to the theme in that prayer, it is often repeated in a very unsystematic way. Before the institution narrative there are numerous requests that God accept, bless, and approve the offering and the gifts. The anamnesis, which petitions that God accept the bread of life and the chalice from the many gifts he has given us, continues with a request that the offerings be accepted as were the sacrificial gifts of Abel, Abraham, and Melchisedech. This is followed by a petition that the sacrifice be taken to the altar in heaven.

Although some restricted use of sacrificial terminology occurs throughout the new Eucharistic Prayers, it is only in conjunction with the anamnesis that there is an explicit statement of offering. Using traditional terminology Prayer II speaks of offering "this life-giving bread, this saving cup," and Prayer III refers to "this holy and living sacrifice." The phraseology of Prayer IV is less traditional speaking as it does of offering Christ's "body and blood." And yet there is a close union between the unique sacrifice of Christ and the sacrificial memorial of the Church which is joined to Christ. What is offered is the Church's sacrifice of praise in the context of the sacramental action of the offering made once and for all by Christ.

Documentation

General Instruction of the Roman Missal, Third Typical Edition

79f. *Offering*: By which, in this very memorial, the Church—and in particular the Church here and now gathered—offers in the Holy Spirit the spotless Victim to the Father. The Church's intention, however, is that the faithful not only offer this spotless Victim but also learn to offer themselves, and so day by day to be consummated, through Christ the Mediator, into unity with God and with each other, so that at last God may be all in all.

Reflection

There is only one offering action in the Mass, and it is celebrated during the Eucharistic Prayer. It is an offering made by the whole Church but especially by the community assembled in faith. In a prayer of praise to the Father the faithful offer themselves with and through Jesus Christ, the pure and holy victim, the High Priest who joins the offering of the Church to his own. "By offering the Immaculate Victim, not only through the hands of the priest, but also with him, they (the faithful) should learn to offer themselves too. Through Christ the Mediator, they should be drawn day by day into ever closer union with God and with each other, so that finally God may be all in all" (Constitution on the Sacred Liturgy, art. 48; see GIRM no. 79f).

Suggested Questions for Discussion
1. In what sense is the Eucharist an offering? A meal?
2. How do people generally understand the Eucharist as an offering?
3. In what ways do the faithful offer themselves with Christ?
4. What is the role of the priest celebrant in the offering presented to the Father?

39
Intercessions

Historical Survey

The Jewish blessing prayer over the cup included various formulas requesting God to show mercy upon the people of Israel, to send Elijah and the Messiah, and to restore the house of David. It is not surprising, therefore, that at an early period the Eucharistic Prayer came to include intercessions for various classes of peoples. Yet these are not part of the earliest tradition of the prayer; they were added only once the main structural elements were in place since they appear at different places in various liturgical traditions. At Antioch these occurred at the end of the prayer, while at Alexandria they were placed before the institution narrative. In the Roman Canon there is a preliminary bloc of intercessions before the institution narrative which mention the Church, the Pope, the local Bishop, certain members of the living, and those assembled. These are followed by a list of the Apostles and Martyrs especially venerated at Rome. Toward the end of the prayer occurs a second set of intercessory prayers which remember the dead and invoke the Martyrs and Saints. The structure of the intercessions in the Roman Canon remains unchanged, although the lists of the Saints may be shortened.

The new Eucharistic Prayers follow the Antiochene tradition and place all the intercessions toward the end of the prayer and link them with the epiclesis. The assembly first requests the fruits of the Eucharist and then prays for more universal intentions. The arrangement of the intercessions, always quite restrained, varies in each prayer, but there is always supplication for the Church and her pastors, for the immediate community and for the dead. The Saints are merely commemorated in Prayers II and IV: Prayer III refers to their "constant intercession."

Documentation

General Instruction of the Roman Missal, Third Typical Edition

79g. *Intercessions*: By which expression is given to the fact that the Eucharist is celebrated in communion with the entire Church, of heaven as well as of earth, and that the offering is made for her and for all her members, living and dead, who have been called to participate in the redemption and the salvation purchased by Christ's Body and Blood.

Reflection

The gathered assembly, having requested the help of the unifying Spirit, quite naturally asks the Father that salvation and redemption be brought not only to its own members but to all, both the living and the dead. In this request the Church unites itself to Christ who "lives forever to make intercession" (Hebrews 7:25). Since the Eucharist is the pledge of future glory, the faithful also recall the Virgin Mary, the Apostles, the Martyrs, and all the Saints who already share in the heavenly banquet announced and prefigured by the Eucharist. The Eucharistic Prayer names only those with whom the ecclesial community shares the faith.

Suggested Questions for Discussion
1. What is the purpose of these intercessions?
2. Do the intentions of the Prayer of the Faithful duplicate them in any way? Should they?

40
Final Doxology

Historical Survey

The traditional conclusion to the Eucharistic Prayer has been a solemn statement of praise and thanksgiving, usually in the form of a trinitarian doxology, to which all respond *Amen*. The value and significance of this *Amen* was attested as early as the mid-second century by Justin who called special attention to it: "When the prayer of thanksgiving is ended, all the people present give their assent with an *Amen*" (*I Apologia* 65:3).

In the ancient papal liturgy the archdeacon lifted the chalice by its handles during the concluding formula. The Pope touched the cup with the consecrated bread or simply elevated the latter. This gesture lasted throughout the entire doxology until the final acclamation of the people. The Middle Ages saw this action diminish with the introduction of various signs of the cross which shortened the duration of the elevation. From the fourteenth century the priest placed the chalice on the altar, genuflected, and then began the *Per omnia saecula saeculorum (For ever and ever)*. These concluding words thus appeared as an introduction to the Our Father which followed.

This formula, sometimes called the "Lesser Doxology," is now restored to its original beauty and importance. The bread and chalice are raised on high in a gesture of offering (this is the gesture of the Eucharistic Prayer) as the doxology is sung or said by the priest. The text is trinitarian, yet with special emphasis on Christ as the mediator. If a deacon is present, it is he who elevates the chalice. The whole congregation, as a priestly people, acclaims *Amen* as a sign of support and adherence.

Documentation

General Instruction of the Roman Missal, Third Typical Edition

79h. *Final doxology*: By which the glorification of God is expressed and is confirmed and concluded by the people's acclamation, *Amen*.

151. … At the end of the Eucharistic Prayer, the priest takes the paten with the host and the chalice and elevates them both while alone singing or saying the doxology, *Per ipsum (Through him)*. At the end the people make the acclamation, *Amen*. Then the priest places the paten and the chalice on the corporal.

Music in Catholic Worship

58. The worshippers assent to the eucharistic prayer and make it their own in the Great Amen. To be most effective, the Amen may be repeated or augmented. Choirs may harmonize and expand upon the people's acclamation.

Reflection

The final doxology summarizes the Eucharistic Prayer which concludes, as it began, on an explicit note of praise. The Church offers praise and honor to the Father through Christ who is the High Priest, with Christ who is really present in the sacrificial memorial, and in Christ who gives himself in the Eucharist to the members of his body. The Church at prayer is united to the Holy Spirit who accomplishes the epiphany of Christ's sacramental and ecclesial body. The priest proclaims the Eucharistic Prayer in the name of the congregation which confirms and approves this action by its *Amen*—more or less equivalent in Hebrew to the English expression "So be it"—given in energetic song or in a loud voice as befits this primary acclamation of the eucharistic celebration.

Suggested Questions for Discussion

1. What is the purpose of the final doxology?
2. When is it sung? Recited?
3. By whom is it to be sung or recited?
4. What is the meaning of the gesture which accompanies the doxology?
5. How long should it last?
6. What is the purpose of the congregation's *Amen*?
7. How may it be augmented?
8. When the doxology and *Amen* are sung, how is musical continuity effected?

C. Communion Rite

41
General Overview

Historical Survey

In the earliest celebrations of the Eucharist the bishop had no fixed formula to say after the people's *Amen* which concluded the Eucharistic Prayer. Once the bread was broken, ministers and faithful received the Body and Blood of the Lord.

The growing desire to express such dispositions as mutual love, unity, and forgiveness resulted in an initial expansion before the reception of the Eucharist. By the early fifth century the Lord's Prayer and—in some churches—the sharing of the peace were established parts of the rite, although the sequence of these elements was not the same in every liturgical tradition. The following centuries saw the addition of other expressive ceremonies and prayers. The whole rite was also subject to various liturgical revisions which changed the position of its components. The result was a rather complex ritual somewhat elusive as regards its inner logic. Although the Order of Mass has not substantially reduced the number of these elements, it has at least arranged them into a more comprehensible pattern.

The actual Communion of ministers and people long remained quite simple. From at least the third century a short formula accompanied the faithful's reception of the Eucharist, a practice which at Rome seems to have fallen into disuse by the early Middle Ages. By the sixth century a song to accompany the procession was added. It seems that it was only outside Rome and beginning about the tenth century that various formulas to introduce and accompany the Communion of priest and people gradually entered various liturgical books. But by the thirteenth century Communion by the faithful, other than at the moment of death, was on the point of disappearing. Theologians and preachers reacted by stressing the need for frequent Communion. At the same time the rites of preparation for Communion apart from Mass, with their formulas of confession and absolution, were inserted as a preliminary to the reception by the faithful within Mass. As a consequence, the Communion Rite came to be separated into two parts, with one set of introductory and accompanying formulas for the priest and another set for the people.

The Order of Mass restores the unity of the Communion Rite by eliminating the various formulas before the people's Communion and by prefacing the Communion of both ministers and people with one introductory formula. The Communion procession and song, now restored, highlight the communal dimensions of the rite.

The need to give a definitive conclusion to the Communion Rite is seen as early as the fifth century with the appearance of the prayer after communion. Starting with the seventh century various forms of purifying the priest's mouth, fingers, and the chalice arose at Rome and elsewhere. The functional task of cleansing is now simplified and may even take place after the celebration to allow both ministers and people an opportunity for prayerful silence or common song before the prayer after communion which serves to conclude the rite.

Documentation

General Instruction of the Roman Missal, Third Typical Edition

80. Since the Eucharistic Celebration is the Paschal Banquet, it is desirable that in keeping with the Lord's command, his Body and Blood should be received by the faithful who are properly disposed as spiritual food. This is the sense of the fraction and the other preparatory rites by which the faithful are led directly to Communion.

Music in Catholic Worship

48. The eating and drinking of the Body and Blood of the Lord in a paschal meal is the climax of our eucharistic celebration. It is prepared for by several rites: the Lord's Prayer with embolism and doxology, the rite of peace, breaking of bread (and commingling) during the "Lamb of God," private preparation of the priest, and showing of the eucharistic bread. The eating and drinking are accompanied by a song expressing the unity of communicants and is followed by a time of prayer after communion (GIRM 56 [80]). Those elements are primary which show forth signs that the first fruit of the Eucharist is the unity of the Body of Christ, Christians being loved by Christ and loving him through their love of one another. The principal texts to accompany or express the sacred action are the Lord's Prayer, the song during the communion procession, and the prayer after communion.

Reflection

The rites of preparation for Communion are a structural link between the Eucharistic Prayers and the reception of the Eucharist. They are rites "by which the faithful are led directly to Communion" (GIRM no. 80). Their purpose is to prepare the whole congregation for its participation in the Lord's Body and Blood. Mutual love and reconciliation are the seeds and fruits of the sacrament shared in communal fashion by ministers and people.

Suggested Questions for Discussion

1. What is the purpose of the rites preparing for communion?
2. To what extent do these rites actually lead the faithful directly to Communion (see GIRM no. 80)?
3. What texts are primary in the Communion Rite?

42
Lord's Prayer

Historical Survey

The Lord's Prayer enjoys a unique place in Christian tradition, spirituality, and worship. Two textual versions are found in the New Testament: Luke 11:24 and Matthew 6:9–13, the latter utilized by the liturgy where the prayer's first three petitions may be seen in close association with the Eucharistic Prayer and its last four petitions (bread and forgiveness) and also, in its present liturgical context, as looking ahead to the Communion.

The prayer entered the liturgy early on: St. Ambrose (c.339–397) mentions its use in Milan. Initially the formula was usually prayed immediately after the breaking of the bread, but St. Gregory the Great (590–604), influenced by St. Augustine (354–430), wanted to link the prayer more closely to the Eucharistic Prayer and so placed it before the "fraction" rite. Contrary to the practice of the east where the Our Father was sung by all the people, in the west the prayer was reserved to the priest with the assembly's intervention of an *Amen* at the end of each petition or, as in the Roman rite, at the very conclusion of the prayer.

The final petition of the Our Father has customarily been followed by an expansion asking the Lord to grant perfect peace. The addition of this request, known as the embolism (from the Greek for "insertion"), may date to the time when the prayer was first introduced in the Mass. The Roman version of the embolism invoked the Virgin Mary and certain apostles especially venerated at Rome.

The Byzantine rite traditionally concludes the Lord's Prayer with the acclamation *For the kingdom, the power, and the glory ....* This doxology seemingly resulted from the desire to end the prayer with a more positive statement than *deliver us from evil*. The antiquity of this acclamation is evident since it is found in some biblical manuscripts, probably as the result of liturgical usage.

Following eastern practice, the Order of Mass calls for the Lord's Prayer to be sung (although it is not inherently a sung element) or recited by the whole congregation. The embolism that follows has been shortened. It is also enriched by the addition of the eschatological words taken from St. Paul's letter to Titus (2:13): "as we await the blessed hope, the appearance of the glory ... of our Savior, Jesus Christ" This serves as a transition to the acclamation "For the kingdom, the power, and the glory are yours, now and forever" which the Order of Mass now introduces into the Roman liturgy.

Documentation

General Instruction of the Roman Missal, Third Typical Edition

81. In the Lord's Prayer a petition is made for daily food, which for Christians means preeminently the eucharistic bread, and also for purification from sin, so that what is holy may, in fact, be given to those who are holy. The priest says the invitation to the prayer, and all the faithful say it with him; the priest alone adds the embolism, which the people conclude with a doxology. The embolism, enlarging upon the last

THE MYSTERY OF FAITH

petition of the Lord's Prayer itself, begs deliverance from the power of evil for the entire community of the faithful.

The invitation, the Prayer itself, the embolism, and the doxology by which the people conclude these things are sung or said aloud.

152. After the Eucharistic Prayer is concluded, the priest, with hands joined, says the introduction to the Lord's Prayer. With hands extended, he then says this prayer together with the people.

153. After the Lord's Prayer is concluded, the priest alone, with hands extended, says the *embolism Libera nos (Deliver us)*. At the end, the people make the acclamation *Quia tuum est regnum (For yours is the kingdom)*.

Music in Catholic Worship

67. This prayer begins our immediate preparation for sharing in the Paschal Banquet. The traditional text is retained and may be set to music by composers with the same freedom as other parts of the Ordinary. All settings must provide for the participation of the priest and all present.

59. These words of praise, "For the Kingdom, the power and the glory are yours, now and forever," are fittingly sung by all, especially when the Lord's Prayer is sung. Here, too, the choir may enhance the acclamation with harmony.

Reflection

The Lord's Prayer is a petition "for daily food, which for Christians means preeminently the eucharistic bread, and also for purification from sin, so that what is holy may in fact, be given to those who are holy" (GIRM no. 81). As such it begins the community's preparation for sharing in the Eucharist. After the priest paraphrases the final petition and introduces the note of peace and expectation, the people give the doxological acclamation *For the kingdom …* which in turn is thematically linked to the Lord's Prayer with its request for the complete realization of God's reign.

Suggested Questions for Discussion

1. What themes of the Our Father make this prayer appropriate as a preparation for Communion?
2. May the priest modify its invitation according to the occasion?
3. What gesture is used by the priest during this prayer? What is its meaning?
4. Are any gestures used by the congregation during the prayer? If so, how appropriate are they? What do they signify?
5. Is the Lord's Prayer ever sung? If so, how often? By whom?
6. What types of musical settings are effective?
7. If the Lord's Prayer is sung, should the embolism and the doxology also be sung?
8. What is the purpose of the embolism?
9. What does the embolism add to the prayer?
10. What is the purpose of the doxology?

43
Rite of Peace

Historical Survey

Among early Christians the kiss of peace was seen as a seal placed on prayer. This gesture soon passed into the liturgy and at Rome occurred after the Prayer of the Faithful which concluded the Liturgy of the Word. In such a position the kiss of peace was also viewed as a sign of that mutual love required by Christ (see Matthew 5:23–24) before offering sacrifice. Some time before Innocent I (401–417)—we do not know exactly when—Rome placed the kiss of peace immediately after the Our Father, a position already known by St. Augustine (354–430) in Africa. Pope Innocent I (d. 417) defended its new location "as a sign of the people's acquiescence in all that has been done in these mysteries" *(Epistola 25 Decentio Augubino 1,* 4). This position also harmonized with the prayer's last petition that we be forgiven "as we forgive those who trespass against us". Eventually the sign was closely linked with the reception of the Eucharist. It was exchanged when the Eucharist was distributed outside Mass; within Mass it was frequently reserved for those who would be receiving the Sacrament.

The people remained in their places and exchanged the peace with their immediate neighbors. In the early Middle Ages the priest began to kiss the altar, in some places the host or chalice, and then exchanged the sign of peace with his assistants who in turn extended it to the members of the congregation. At this time when frequency of Communion had greatly declined, the sign of peace was even regarded as a kind of substitute for the sacrament. In England it was customary to kiss a small tablet of wood or metal, known as a pax-board, which was passed from one member of the assembly to the other. Gradually the gesture was limited to the clergy alone or completely replaced by the priest's kissing of the altar. In Frankish lands the exchange was introduced by a prayer for peace said by the priest. The formula *Lord Jesus Christ* dates from the eleventh century and was prescribed by the Missal of Pius V (1570) even when the peace was not exchanged. In these cases it was generally understood as one of the priest's private prayers of preparation for communion.

Today the priest with extended hands says aloud the prayer *Lord Jesus Christ*. The wish for peace with the people's answer follows. Next the deacon or, in his absence, the priest may and normally should request all to share the peace with one another. Since the peace is to be exchanged with persons who are rather close by, "neither the people nor the ministers need try exhaust the sign by attempting to give the greeting personally to everyone in the congregation or even to a great number of those present … Unless the sign of peace is clearly tailored to a specific occasion, such as a marriage, ordination, or some small intimate group, the more elaborate and individual exchange of peace by the celebrant has a tendency to appear clumsy. It can also accentuate too much the role of the celebrant or ministers, which runs counter to a true understanding of the presence of Christ in the entire assembly" (Bishops' Committee on the Liturgy: *The Sign of Peace,* 1977).

Documentation
General Instruction of the Roman Missal, Third Typical Edition

82. The Rite of Peace follows, by which the Church asks for peace and unity for herself and for the whole human family, and the faithful express to each other their ecclesial communion and mutual charity before communicating in the Sacrament.

    As for the sign of peace to be given, the manner is to be established by Conferences of Bishops in accordance with the culture and customs of the peoples. It is, however, appropriate that each person offer the sign of peace only to those who are nearest and in a sober manner.

154. Then the priest, with hands extended, says aloud the prayer, *Domine Iesu Christe, qui dixisti (Lord Jesus Christ, you said)*. After this prayer is concluded, extending and then joining his hands, he gives the greeting of peace while facing the people and saying, *Pax Domini sit simper vobiscum (The peace of the Lord be with you always)*. The people answer, *Et cum spiritu tuo (And also with you)*. Afterwards, when appropriate, the priest adds, *Offerte vobis pacem (Let us offer each other the sign of peace)*.

    The priest may give the sign of peace to the ministers but always remains within the sanctuary, so as not to disturb the celebration. In the dioceses of the United States of America, for a good reason, on special occasions (for example, in the case of a funeral, a wedding, or when civic leaders are present) the priest may offer the sign of peace to a few of the faithful near the sanctuary. At the same time, in accord with the decisions of the Conference of Bishops, all offer one another a sign that expresses peace, communion, and charity. While the sign of peace is being given, one may say, *Pax Domini sit semper vobiscum (The peace of the Lord be with you always)*, to which the response is *Amen*.

Reflection

The Hebrew word for peace is *shalom*, namely all possible prosperity, the state of a person who lives in complete harmony with nature, self, and God. Since the risen Christ is the source of all peace, this gesture expresses faith that Christ is present in his people . It is both a call to reconciliation, unity, and communion, as well as a seal which ratifies the very meaning of a eucharistic assembly whose members both find and pray for peace in one another.

Suggested Questions for Discussion

1. What is the purpose of the Rite of Peace?
2. Do people understand its meaning?
3. What is the relationship between this rite and the Act of Penitence at the beginning of the celebration?
4. What is the relationship of this rite and the proclamation of the Scriptures which call the community to reconciliation?
5. Should the sign of peace always be exchanged?
6. How long should the exchange of peace last?
7. Do people enjoy exchanging the peace?
8. With whom should the sign be exchanged?

44
Breaking of Bread

Historical Survey

Conforming to the rite of the Passover meal, Christ took bread into his hands, pronounced the prayer of praise, and then broke the bread. Primitively this breaking of the bread was the only rite that occurred between the Eucharistic Prayer and the Communion. The gesture was soon seen as a sign of unity: participating in the one bread which is broken, all form one body in Christ (see 1 Corinthians 10:17). In fact, the Eucharist itself was once called "the breaking of the bread" (see Acts 2:42). As the numbers of Christians increased the action became quite elaborate. In the papal liturgy the Pope presided at his chair while the assisting priest and subdeacons broke the loaves of bread for the Communion of the faithful. But with the adoption of unleavened bread in the west and with the subsequent introduction of small hosts for the people, the prominence of the rite greatly diminished. The breaking was joined to the commingling, and the priest alone consumed the large host.

The Order of Mass strives to highlight the symbolic meaning of the rite. Although small breads consecrated at the same celebration may also be used, care is to be taken that at least some of the people receive portions from the large host(s) broken at this time. The deacon may assist at the breaking.

Documentation

General Instruction of the Roman Missal, Third Typical Edition

83. The priest breaks the Eucharistic Bread, assisted, if the case calls for it, by the deacon or a concelebrant. Christ's gesture of breaking bread at the Last Supper, which gave the entire Eucharistic Action its name in apostolic times, signifies that the many faithful are made one body (1 Cor 10:17) by receiving Communion from the one Bread of Life which is Christ, who died and rose for the salvation of the world. The fraction or breaking of bread is begun after the sign of peace and is carried out with proper reverence, though it should not be unnecessarily prolonged, nor should it be accorded undue importance. This rite is reserved to the priest and the deacon. …

321. The meaning of the sign demands that the material for the Eucharistic celebration truly have the appearance of food. It is therefore expedient that the Eucharistic bread, even though unleavened and baked in the traditional shape, be made in such a way that the priest at Mass with a congregation is able in practice to break it into parts for distribution to at least some of the faithful. Small hosts are, however, in no way ruled out when the number of those receiving Holy Communion or other pastoral needs require it. The action of the fraction or breaking of bread, which gave its name to the Eucharist in apostolic times, will bring out more clearly the force and importance of the sign of unity of all in the one bread, and of the sign of

charity by the fact that the one bread is distributed among the brothers and sisters.

Norms for the Distribution and Reception of Holy Communion Under Both Kinds in the Dioceses of the United States of America (Revised 2004)

37. As the *Agnus Dei* or *Lamb of God* is begun, the Bishop or priest alone, or with the assistance of the deacon, and if necessary of concelebrating priests, breaks the eucharistic bread. Other empty ciboria or patens are then brought to the altar is this is necessary. The deacon or priest places the consecrated bread in several ciboria or patens, if necessary, as required for the distribution of Holy Communion. If it is not possible to accomplish this distribution in a reasonable time, the celebrant may call upon the assistance of other deacons or concelebrating priests.

Reflection

The classic explanation of the breaking and sharing of the one bread is given by St. Paul: "The bread that we break, is it not a participation in the body of Christ? Because the loaf of bread is one, we, though many, are one body, for we all partake of the one loaf" (1 Corinthians 10:16b–17). Christ gives to all the one bread which is his body. Just as this bread has become the body of Christ, so those who share this one bread, whatever be their diversity, become one body in Christ. In the words of the *Didache*, an anonymous document dating from the second or third centuries: "As this broken bread, scattered over the mountains, was gathered together to be one, so may your Church be gathered together in the same manner from the ends of the earth into your kingdom …"

Suggested Questions for Discussion

1. What is the meaning of the breaking of the Eucharistic bread?
2. Do people see this action taking place?
3. How does the texture of the bread affect the act of breaking?
4. Who may assist the priest in breaking the bread?
5. Where does this action take place?
6. How long should it take?
7. How much of the Eucharistic bread should be broken at this point in the celebration when the congregation is very large?
8. Why is the bread broken over the paten rather than over the chalice as formerly?

45
Commingling

Historical Survey

The Roman Mass has historically known various commingling rites, each considered as expressing some aspect of unity. At Rome a priest, who for pastoral reasons was unable to celebrate with the pope, received a small piece of bread, called the *fermentum*, which was consecrated at the papal liturgy (we don't know when this practice was first introduced). The priest then placed this particle in his own chalice as a sign of unity with the Pope. At one period of history the continuity of the eucharistic Sacrifice was symbolized by the priest's placing into the chalice a particle of bread consecrated at a previous celebration.

The present commingling, however, originates from a rite introduced into the Roman Mass, according to some historians, by a Syrian pope in the first half of the eighth century. An extremely realistic theology of the Eucharist arose in Syria. Just as the double consecration, i.e., of the bread and of the wine, represented the death of Christ, so it was deemed necessary to symbolize the resurrection which ensures the bread of immortality received in Communion. This took place by reuniting the Body and Blood before the Communion, a kind of symbolic reenactment of the Lord's resurrection. A prayer dating from the middle of the eighth century was added to the rite in the west.

The Order of Mass retains both the rite and a modified version of the prayer which is said quietly.

Documentation

General Instruction of the Roman Missal, Third Typical Edition

83. … The priest breaks the Bread and puts a piece of the host into the chalice to signify the unity of the Body and Blood of the Lord in the work of salvation, namely, of the living and glorious Body of Jesus Christ.

155. The priest then takes the host and breaks it over the paten. He places a small piece in the chalice, saying quietly, *Haec commixtio (May the mingling)*. Meanwhile the *Agnus Dei* is sung or said by the choir and congregation …

Reflection

Since the commingling rite appears in all the eastern liturgies, it may have been retained for ecumenical reasons. Or perhaps simply for the sake of tradition. The accompanying prayer requests the fruits of Communion.

Suggested Questions for Discussion

1. What is the purpose of the commingling rite?
2. Do people ever notice it?
3. How do they understand it?
4. Should it be emphasized?
5. In what manner is the accompanying prayer said?

46
"Lamb of God"

Historical Survey

The breaking of the bread was especially lengthy in the papal liturgy. It was, therefore, accompanied by the singing of a chant which originally might have been variable. Pope Sergius I (687–701) is said to have introduced the *Lamb of God* to fill out the rite. Being Syrian, Sergius probably borrowed this chant from the Syrian liturgy. Its text is taken from the acknowledgment given Jesus by John the Baptist (see John 1:23, 36): Christ is the Paschal Lamb (see 1 Corinthians 5:7, John 19:36) who has conquered death (see Revelation 5:6; 13:8).

The chant was originally sung by the people and the assisting clergy and was seemingly repeated as often as necessary to accompany the action. With the development of complex melodies it was gradually reserved to the choir. As the number of communicants decreased and as unleavened hosts replaced leavened bread, the action of breaking the bread became quite brief. As a result the text came to be sung only three times. The wording was originally unchanged at each repetition. But from the tenth century the last phrase was changed to "grant us peace," probably the result of linking the chant to the kiss of peace which in the ninth century began to be transferred from before to after breaking of the bread.

Today the *Lamb of God* is restored as a chant to accompany the breaking of the bread and the commingling. It may, therefore, be repeated as often as necessary. It is a litany-song of the choir, cantor, and/or congregation and not of the priest who is engaged in the action of breaking.

Documentation

General Instruction of the Roman Missal, Third Typical Edition

83. The priest breaks the Eucharistic Bread, assisted, if the case calls for it, by the deacon or a concelebrant. Christ's gesture of breaking bread at the Last Supper, which gave the entire Eucharistic Action its name in apostolic times, signifies that the many faithful are made one body (1 Cor 10:17) by receiving Communion from the one Bread of Life which is Christ, who died and rose for the salvation of the world. The fraction or breaking of bread is begun after the sign of peace and is carried out with proper reverence, though it should not be unnecessarily prolonged, nor should it be accorded undue importance. This rite is reserved to the priest and the deacon.

    The priest breaks the Bread and puts a piece of the host into the chalice to signify the unity of the Body and Blood of the Lord in the work of salvation, namely, of the living and glorious Body of Jesus Christ. The supplication *Agnus Dei*, is, as a rule, sung by the choir or cantor with the congregation responding; or it is, at least, recited aloud. This invocation accompanies the fraction and, for this reason, may be repeated as many times as necessary until the rite has reached its conclusion, the last time ending with the words *dona nobis pacem (grant us peace)*.

155. The priest then takes the host and breaks it over the paten. He places a small piece in the chalice, saying quietly, *Haec commixtio (May the mingling)*. Meanwhile the *Agnus Dei* is sung or said by the choir and congregation …

43. … The faithful kneel after the *Agnus Dei* unless the Diocesan Bishop determines otherwise.

Music in Catholic Worship

68. The Agnus Dei is a litany-song to accompany the breaking of the bread in preparation for communion. The invocation and response may be repeated as the action demands. The final response is always "grant us peace." Unlike the "Holy, Holy, Holy Lord," and the Lord's Prayer, the "Lamb of God" is not necessarily a song of the people. Hence it may be sung by the choir, though the people should generally make the response.

Liturgical Music Today

20. The Lamb of God achieves greater significance at Masses when a larger sized eucharistic bread is broken for distribution and, when communion is given under both kinds, chalices must be filled. The litany is prolonged to accompany this action of breaking and pouring (GIRM 56e [83]). In this case one should not hesitate to add tropes to the litany so that the prayerfulness of the rite may be enriched.

Reflection

The *Lamb of God* is a litany song designed to accompany an action. Hence its function is evident only when there is bread to be broken. Jesus is the Lamb of the new Covenant. We "were ransomed … with the precious blood of Christ as of a spotless, unblemished lamb" (1 Peter 1:18–19). Every Eucharist is a memorial of the new Passover which brings forgiveness of sin, peace of mind and soul.

Suggested Questions for Discussion

1. What is the purpose of the Lamb of God?
2. Does its text express the meaning of the action it accompanies?
3. Why does the text conclude with "grant us peace"?
4. What is the purpose of the Lamb of God when the fraction is of minimal length?
5. Who intones the Lamb of God?
6. Does the priest join the rest of the congregation in singing or reciting the text?
7. How often is the text sung? When should it be sung? By whom?
8. What should be the "feel" of a sung Lamb of God? Praise? Simple petition? Urgent pleading?
9. Does a gesture accompany the "have mercy on us"?

47
Private Preparation of Priest and People

Historical Survey
It was in France that various prayers recited by the priest before Communion appeared during the Middle Ages. Said silently, frequently addressed to Christ, and often written in the first person plural, they were meant as private prayers to foster the devotion of the priest celebrant. The Missal of Pius V (1570) required the priest to say a prayer for peace not only at Solemn High Masses, the only occasion when the peace was exchanged and then only among the clergy, but also at all other Masses. Two additional prayers were also selected from among the numerous formulas which appeared in the medieval liturgical books to stimulate the piety of the priest before Communion.

All three prayers are retained today although with a different disposition. The first formula now introduces the rite of peace. The second and third remain as a preparation for Communion, but the priest may choose one of the two. Being private prayers, they are always said inaudibly.

Documentation
General Instruction of the Roman Missal, Third Typical Edition
84. The priest prepares himself by a prayer, said quietly, that he may fruitfully receive Christ's Body and Blood. The faithful do the same, praying silently …
156. Then the priest, with hands joined, quietly says the preparatory prayer of Communion: *Domine Iesu Christe, Fili Dei vivi (Lord Jesus Christ, Son of the living God)* or *Perceptio Corporis et Sanguinis (Lord Jesus Christ, with faith in your love and mercy).*

Reflection
Since the prayers of the priest are to be said inaudibly, each member of the congregation is now offered an opportunity for individual and silent prayer before Communion. The prayer of the priest is not to supplant the silent preparation of the people.

Suggested Questions for Discussion
1. What is the purpose of this time of preparation?
2. Is the congregation aware of its purpose?
3. Why is the prayer of the priest said inaudibly?

48
Invitation to Communion

Historical Survey

Various prayers introducing the Communion of the priest and the congregation entered the Mass in the Middle Ages and were only prescribed and standardized in the sixteenth century. Until 1969 the priest said a series of short prayers as he took and received the body of Christ; two prayers accompanied his reception from the chalice. If the assembly was to receive the Eucharist, the *Confiteor* and formulas of absolution followed. The priest then gave the invitation "Behold the Lamb of God … " and repeated three times "Lord, I am not worthy …"

Today there is one invitation which precedes the Communion of both priest and people. The rite has thus been simplified, and all the formulas are taken from Scripture. The priest shows the Eucharistic Bread to the people as he says aloud "This is the Lamb of God who takes away the sins of the world" (cf. John 1:29) to which is added words that are drawn from those of the angel in Revelation 19:9 "Blessed are those who have been called to the wedding feast of the Lamb". This invitation may be adapted to the feast or occasion. Since all share in one and the same Eucharist, both priest and people respond "Lord, I am not worthy to receive you but only say the word and I shall be healed" (cf. Matthew 8:8).

Documentation

General Instruction of the Roman Missal, Third Typical Edition

84. … The priest next shows the faithful the Eucharistic Bread, holding it above the paten or above the chalice, and invites them to the banquet of Christ. Along with the faithful, he then makes an act of humility using the prescribed words taken from the Gospels.

157. When the prayer is concluded, the priest genuflects, takes the host consecrated in the same Mass, and, holding it slightly raised above the paten or above the chalice, while facing the people, says, *Ecce Agnus Dei (This is the Lamb of God)*. With the people he adds, *Domine, non sum dignus (Lord, I am not worthy)*.

Reflection

A formal invitation to receive the Lord's Body and Blood is found in almost every traditional liturgy. One of the popular forms used in the east is "Holy things to the Holy!" The present Roman form strikes a balance between a worthiness rooted in Baptism and a humility possessed by the centurion. The congregation is invited to look at the Eucharistic Bread and to express reverence, confidence, and faith.

Suggested Questions for Discussion

1. What is the purpose of the invitation to Communion?
2. In what manner is the invitation given?
3. Does a gesture accompany the words "Lord, I am not worthy"?

49
Distribution of the Eucharist

Historical Survey

Although in early Christianity both Bishop and people simply consumed the consecrated elements in silence, the need to verbalize the meaning of this action soon resulted in various formulas accompanying the distribution of the Eucharist, at least to the faithful. One text used in Syria, Africa, and Rome was *The Body of Christ* to which the communicant responded with a profession of faith, the *Amen*. In parts of the east the initial formula was at times expanded, and the minister often addressed each one, if possible, by the person's baptismal name. By the early Middle Ages, however, Rome seems to have lost the custom of distributing communion with an accompanying formula.

It was outside Rome and in the tenth century that there again appeared formulas, all somewhat similar in wording, designed to accompany the rite. These were blessings or wishes rather than professions of faith calling for the involvement of the communicant. At the same time liturgical books began to incorporate prayers to accompany the priest's Communion. The Missal of 1570 standardized and prescribed these texts. A short set of formulas, each concluding with a petition that the Eucharist keep the priest's soul unto everlasting life, preceded his reception of both the eucharistic bead and wine. While distributing the Lord's Body to each of the faithful the priest was to say *May the Body of our Lord Jesus Christ keep your soul unto life everlasting*, and he was also to add the response *Amen*.

Today the presiding priest, as leader of the celebration and in accord with ancient usage, remains the first to receive the consecrated bread and wine, each time saying what is substantially the same concluding petition found in the former Missal. And just as Christ at the Last Supper "gave" his Body and Blood to the Apostles, so it has been traditional that a minister present the Eucharist to the faithful. Before distributing the Lord's body to each communicant, the minister shows the host to each person by raising it a little above the paten and says "The Body of Christ." The communicant answers "Amen" and receives the bread of life. A similar formula "The Blood of Christ" precedes the reception from the chalice.

For numerous centuries Christians carried out in literal fashion Christ's command to "take and eat … take and drink." Receiving the Eucharist under both kinds was normative: to refuse the chalice was considered a sign of heresy or superstition. And yet the reception of the Eucharist under one form alone was accepted under special circumstances, e.g., when a person was very ill or when infants baptized and confirmed during the Easter Vigil received the Eucharist only under the form of wine.

But by the early fourteenth century communion under both kinds was becoming the exception rather than the rule. This was the result of a number of changes in religious piety and understanding which occurred in previous centuries: emphasis on *seeing* the Eucharist with the result that the chalice and its contents (which could not be seen) were considered an auxiliary and secondary element; fear of spillage and disease; the change from standing to kneeling while receiving the sacrament—kneeling being a posture which did not facilitate giving communion from the chalice; the doctrine of concomitance which correctly taught that the whole Christ is totally present under the form of bread and under the form of wine. Several reform groups, however, held that Communion under both kinds was indispensable for salvation. The Council of Trent (1562) reacted by justifying the omission of the lay chalice not as an ideal but on the basis of excusing causes, especially the need for refutation of doctrinal error.

With the subsiding of doctrinal disputes and as a result of a greater appreciation of the symbolism of the Eucharist, The Second Vatican Council initiated a gradual extension once again of the Church's ancient practice of distributing the Eucharist under both kinds to the members of the congregation. Today, in addition to a number of occasions when universal liturgical law permits Communion under both kinds, the diocesan Bishop may make further determinations for his own diocese.

For many centuries the faithful received the eucharistic bread in their hands. But in the Middle Ages this custom was abandoned due to a piety that emphasized the Sacrament as God's awesome gift descending from on high. As a result the eucharistic bread was placed on the communicant's tongue. Permission is given to national Conferences of Bishops to allow the faithful the option of receiving either in the hand (what many consider a very natural and human action) or on the tongue—this option has been allowed in the United States since 1977.

Recent directives have limited the ministry of special or extraordinary ministers of the Eucharist. Rather than, as formerly, assisting at the breaking of the bread and the preparation of the cup, they now enter the sanctuary only after the Communion of the priest, thus during the opening measures of the Communion song. A priest, assisted if necessary by a deacon, distributes communion to them. Then the priest, who may be assisted by a deacon, hands them the vessels. They then proceed to distribute Communion to the rest of the faithful.

The norm for the United States is that communicants are to receive Communion while standing. As a sign of reverence the communicant bows his or her head before receiving the eucharistic bread.

Documentation

General Instruction of the Roman Missal, Third Typical Edition

85. It is most desirable that the faithful, just as the priest himself is bound to do, receive the Lord's Body from hosts consecrated at the same Mass and that, in the instances when it is permitted, they partake of the chalice (cf. below, no. 283), so that even by means of the signs Communion will stand out more clearly as a participation in the sacrifice actually being celebrated.

158. After this, standing and turned toward the altar, the priest says quietly, *Corpus Christi custodiat me in vitam aeternam (May the Body of Christ bring me to everlasting life)* and reverently receives the Body of Christ. Then he takes the chalice, saying quietly, *Sanguis Christi custodiat me in vitam aeternam (May the Blood of Christ bring me to everlasting life)*, and reverently receives the Blood of Christ.

160. The priest then takes the paten or ciborium and goes to the communicants, who, as a rule, approach in a procession.
    The faithful are not permitted to take the consecrated bread or the sacred chalice by themselves and, still less, to hand them from one to another. The norm for reception of Holy Communion in the dioceses of the United States is standing. Communicants should not be denied Holy Communion because they kneel. Rather, such instances should be addressed pastorally, by providing the faithful with proper catechesis on the reasons for this norm.
    When receiving Holy Communion, the communicant bows his or her head before the Sacrament as a gesture of reverence and receives the Body of the Lord from the minister. The consecrated host may be received either on the tongue or in the hand, at the discretion of each communicant. When Holy Communion is received under both kinds, the sign of reverence is also made before receiving the Precious Blood.

161. If Communion is given only under the species of bread, the priest raises the host slightly and shows it to each, saying, *Corpus Christi (The Body of Christ)*. The communicant replies, Amen, and receives the Sacrament either on the tongue or, where this is allowed and if the communicant so chooses, in the hand. As soon as the communicant receives the host, he or she consumes it entirely.
    If, however, Communion is given under both kinds, the rite prescribed in nos. 284-287 is followed.

162. The priest may be assisted in the distribution of Communion by other priests who happen to be present. If such priests are not present and there is a very large number of communicants, the priest may call upon extraordinary ministers to assist him, e.g., duly instituted acolytes or even other faithful who have been deputed for this purpose. In case of necessity, the priest may depute suitable faithful for this single occasion.
    These ministers should not approach the altar before the priest has received Communion, and they are always to receive from the hands of the priest celebrant the vessel containing either species of the Most Holy Eucharist for distribution to the faithful.

281. Holy Communion has a fuller form as a sign when it is distributed under both kinds. For in this form the sign of the eucharistic banquet is more clearly evident and clear expression is given to the divine will by which the new and eternal Covenant is ratified in the Blood of the Lord, as also the relationship between the Eucharistic banquet and the eschatological banquet in the Father's Kingdom.

282. Sacred pastors should take care to ensure that the faithful who participate in the rite or are present at it are as fully aware as possible of the Catholic teaching on the form of Holy Communion as set forth by the Ecumenical Council of Trent. Above all, they should instruct the Christian faithful that the Catholic faith teaches that Christ, whole and entire, and the true Sacrament, is received even under only one species, and consequently that as far as the effects are concerned, those who receive under only one species are not deprived of any of the grace that is necessary for salvation.

They are to teach, furthermore, that the Church, in her stewardship of the Sacraments, has the power to set forth or alter whatever provisions, apart from the substance of the Sacraments, that she judges to be most conducive to the veneration of the Sacraments and the well-being of the recipients, in view of changing conditions, times, and places. At the same time, the faithful should be encouraged to seek to participate more eagerly in this sacred rite, by which the sign of the Eucharistic banquet is made more fully evident.

283. In addition to those cases given in the ritual books, Communion under both kinds is permitted for
   a) Priests who are not able to celebrate or concelebrate Mass;
   b) The deacon and others who perform some duty at the Mass;
   c) Members of communities at the conventual Mass or "community" Mass, along with seminarians, and all who are engaged in a retreat or are taking part in a spiritual or pastoral gathering.

   The Diocesan Bishop may establish norms for Communion under both kinds for his own diocese, which are also to be observed in churches of religious and at celebrations with small groups. The Diocesan Bishop is also given the faculty to permit Communion under both kinds whenever it may seem appropriate to the priest to whom, as its own shepherd, a community has been entrusted, provided that the faithful have been well instructed and there is no danger of profanation of the Sacrament or of the rite's becoming difficult because of the large number of participants or some other reason.

   In all that pertains to Communion under both kinds, the Norms for the Distribution and Reception of Holy Communion under Both Kinds in the Dioceses of the United States of America are to be followed (see nos. 27-54).

284. When Communion is distributed under both kinds,
   a) The chalice is usually administered by a deacon or, when no deacon is present, by a priest, or even by a duly instituted acolyte or another extraordinary minister of Holy Communion, or by a member of the faithful who in case of necessity has been entrusted with this duty for a single occasion; ...

   Any of the faithful who wish to receive Holy Communion under the species of bread alone should be granted their wish.

285. For Communion under both kinds the following should be prepared:
   a) If Communion from the chalice is carried out by communicants' drinking directly from the chalice, a chalice of a sufficiently large size or several chalices are prepared. Care should, however, be taken in planning lest beyond what is needed of the Blood of Christ remains to be consumed at the end of the celebration.
   b) If Communion is carried out by intinction, the hosts should be neither too thin nor too small, but rather a little thicker than usual, so that after being dipped partly into the Blood of Christ they can still easily be distributed to each communicant.

286. If Communion of the Blood of Christ is carried out by communicants' drinking from the chalice, each communicant, after receiving the Body of Christ, moves and

stands facing the minister of the chalice. The minister says, *Sanguis Christi (The Blood of Christ)*, the communicant responds, *Amen*, and the minister hands over the chalice, which the communicant raises to his or her mouth. Each communicant drinks a little from the chalice, hands it back to the minister, and then withdraws; the minister wipes the rim of the chalice with the purificator.

Norms for the Distribution and Reception of Holy Communion Under Both Kinds ...

38. If extraordinary ministers of Holy Communion are required by pastoral need, they approach the altar as the priest receives Communion. After the priest has concluded his own Communion, he distributes Communion to the extraordinary ministers, assisted by the deacon, and then hands the sacred vessels to them for distribution of Holy Communion to the people.

39. All receive Holy Communion in the manner described by the *General Instruction to* (sic) *the Roman Missal*, whether priest concelebrants (cf. GIRM, nos. 159, 242, 243, 246), deacons (cf. GIRM, nos. 182, 244, 246), or extraordinary ministers of Holy Communion (cf. GIRM, no. 284). Neither deacons nor lay ministers may ever receive Holy Communion in the manner of a concelebrating priest. The practice of extraordinary ministers of Holy Communion waiting to receive Holy Communion until after the distribution of Holy Communion is not in accord with liturgical law.

40. After all eucharistic ministers have received Communion, the bishop or priest celebrant reverently hands vessels containing the Body or the Blood of the Lord to the deacons or extraordinary ministers who will assist with the distribution of Holy Communion. The deacon may assist the priest in handing the vessels containing the Body and Blood of the Lord to the extraordinary ministers of Holy Communion.

41. Holy Communion under the form of bread is offered to the communicant with the words "The Body of Christ." The communicant may choose whether to receive the Body of Christ in the hand or on the tongue. When receiving in the hand, the communicant should be guided by the words of St. Cyril of Jerusalem: "When you approach, take care not to do so with your hand stretched out and your fingers open or apart, but rather place your left hand as a throne beneath your right, as befits one who is about to receive the King. Then receive him, taking care that nothing is lost." (Cat. Myst. V, 21-22)

42. Among the ways of ministering the Precious Blood as prescribed by the *General Instruction of the Roman Missal*, Communion from the chalice is generally the preferred form in the Latin Church, provided that it can be carried out properly according to the norms and without any risk of even apparent irreverence toward the Blood of Christ. (Cf. Sacred Congregation for Divine Worship, *Sacramentali Communione*: Instruction Extending the Practice of Communion Under Both Kinds [June 29, 1970], no. 6 [DOL 270, no. 2115])

43. The chalice is offered to the communicant with the words "The Blood of Christ," to which the communicant responds, "Amen."

44. The chalice may never be left on the altar or another place to be picked up by the communicant for self-communication (except in the case of concelebrating bishops or priests), nor may the chalice be passed from one communicant to another. There shall always be a minister of the chalice.

45. After each communicant has received the Blood of Christ, the minister carefully wipes both sides of the rim of the chalice with a purificator. This action is a matter of both reverence and hygiene. For the same reason, the minister turns the chalice slightly after each communicant has received the Precious Blood.
46. It is the choice of the communicant, not the minister, to receive from the chalice.
47. Children are encouraged to receive Communion under both kinds provided that they are properly instructed and that they are old enough to receive from the chalice.
48. Distribution of the Precious Blood by a spoon or through a straw is not customary in the Latin dioceses of the United States of America.
49. Holy Communion may be distributed by intinction in the following manner: "the communicant, while holding the paten under the chin, approaches the priest who holds the vessel with the hosts and at whose side stands the minister holding the chalice. The priest takes the host, intincts the particle into the chalice and showing it, says: 'The Body and Blood of Christ.' The communicant responds, 'Amen,' and receives the Sacrament on the tongue from the priest. Afterwards, the communicant returns to his or her place." (GIRM 287)
50. The communicant, including the extraordinary minister, is never allowed to self-communicate, even by means of intinction. Communion under either form, bread or wine, must always be given by an ordinary or extraordinary minister of Holy Communion.

Instruction "Inaestimabile Donum" on Certain Norms Concerning Worship of the Eucharistic Mystery

9. Eucharistic Communion. Communion is a gift of the Lord, given to the faithful through the minister appointed for this purpose. It is not permitted that the faithful should themselves pick up the consecrated bread and the sacred chalice; still less that they should hand them from one to another.
11. The church has always required from the faithful respect and reverence for the Eucharist at the moment of receiving it.
With regard to the manner of going to Communion, the faithful can receive it either kneeling or standing, in accordance with the norms laid down by the episcopal conference. When the faithful communicate kneeling, no other sign of reverence towards the Blessed Sacrament is required, since kneeling is itself a sign of adoration. When they receive Communion standing, it is strongly recommended that, coming up in procession, they should make a sign of reverence before receiving the sacrament. This should be done at the right time and place, so that the order of people going to and from Communion is not disrupted.

Reflection

As a traditional sign of service to one another a minister, saying *The Body of Christ* and *The Blood of Christ*, presents the eucharistic bread and wine to the communicant. Of special significance is the invitation to receive the Lord's Body since it highlights the importance of the gathered people as the body of Christ. St. Augustine explained the meaning of this phrase: "What is meant by one bread? St. Paul interpreted it briefly: 'We, being many, are one body.' This bread is the body of Christ, to which the Apostle refers when he addressed the Church: Now you are the body of Christ and his members.' That which you receive, that you yourselves are by the grace of the redemption, as you acknowledge when you respond *Amen*. What you witness here is the sacrament of unity" *(Sermo 272)*. The phrase thus expresses the presence of Christ in the Sacrament, in the communicant, and in the whole people. Each person actively responds as a mature individual and professes belief in this presence.

"Holy communion has a fuller form as a sign when it is distributed under both kinds. For in this form the sign of the eucharistic banquet is more clearly evident" (GIRM no. 281). Receiving from the chalice is the sign of the new covenant (see Luke 22:20), the guarantee and expectation of the heavenly banquet (see Mark 26:29), and the sign of union with Christ who suffered (see Mark 10:38–39). Thus "it is most desirable that the faithful … partake of the chalice" (GIRM no. 85).

Suggested Questions for Discussion

1. What is the purpose of the formula accompanying the distribution?
2. What is its meaning?
3. Why are the formulas accompanying the priest's communion said quietly?
4. Does the minister take time to raise the bread and the cup slightly and show them to the communicant?
5. In what manner are the accompanying formulas said?
6. Is it appropriate for the minister to say "This is the Body of Christ"?
7. Is it appropriate for the communicant to respond "Thank you" rather than "Amen"?
8. Why is the action of "giving" by a minister important in the distribution of Communion?
9. May the cup or eucharistic bread be left on the altar for a deacon, extraordinary minister, or other member of the congregation to take by themselves?
10. May others (e.g., cantor, choir members) receive the Eucharist at the same time as the extraordinary ministers?
11. How often is Communion distributed under both kinds? What is the value of receiving from the chalice?
12. What reasons justify distributing eucharistic bread that has been consecrated at a previous celebration?
13. What are the advantages and/or disadvantages of having ushers direct the Communion procession?

50
Music at Communion

Historical Survey

From at least the time of St. Augustine (354–430) it was customary to sing a psalm during the procession of the communicants. One favorite text in both east and west seems to have been Psalm 34, especially because of its ninth verse "Taste and see how good the Lord is." At Rome, which eventually followed in a general way the sequence of the Psalter, the choir and the subdeacons sang in alternation. With the growing length of the sung *Agnus Dei* and perhaps as a result in the decline in the number of communicants, the verses came to be omitted, and the antiphon alone was sung after the Communion.

The Order of Mass restores this ancient chant as an accompaniment to the reception of the Eucharist. Since the Communion of priest and people forms a single rite, the song begins when the priest receives the Sacrament and continues as long as is convenient. Psalm texts are recommended, although other appropriate songs expressive of unity, encounter with the Lord, and joy, chosen in accord with the relevant universal and particular norms, are also appropriate. When there is no singing, the antiphon found in the Missal is recited by the faithful, by a lector, or even by the priest himself *before* he distributes the Eucharist to the people.

Documentation

General Instruction of the Roman Missal, Third Typical Edition

86. While the priest is receiving the Sacrament, the Communion chant is begun. Its purpose is to express the communicants' union in spirit by means of the unity of their voices, to show joy of heart, and to highlight more clearly the "communitarian" nature of the procession to receive Communion. The singing is continued for as long as the Sacrament is being administered to the faithful. If, however, there is to be a hymn after Communion, the Communion chant should be ended in a timely manner.

    Care should be taken that singers, too, can receive Communion with ease.

87. In the dioceses of the United States of America there are four options for the Communion chant: (1) the antiphon from the Roman Missal or the Psalm from the *Roman Gradual* as set to music there or in another musical setting; (2) the seasonal antiphon and Psalm of the *Simple Gradual*; (3) a song from another collection of psalms and antiphons, approved by the United States Conference of Catholic Bishops or the Diocesan Bishop, including psalms arranged in responsorial or metrical forms; (4) a suitable liturgical song chosen in accordance with no. 86 above. This is sung either by the choir alone or by the choir or cantor with the people.

    If there is no singing, however, the Communion antiphon found in the Missal may be recited either by the faithful, or by some of them, or by a lector. Otherwise the priest himself says it after he has received Communion and before he distributes Communion to the faithful.

Music in Catholic Worship

62. The communion song should foster a sense of unity. It should be simple and not demand great effort. It gives expression to the joy of unity in the body of Christ and the fulfillment of the mystery being celebrated. Because they emphasize adoration rather than communion, most benediction hymns are not suitable. In general, during the most important seasons of the Church year—Easter, Lent, Christmas, and Advent—it is preferable that most songs used at the communion be seasonal in nature. During the remainder of the Church year, however, topical songs may be used during the communion procession, provided these texts do not conflict with the paschal character of every Sunday (NCCB, November 1969).

Liturgical Music Today

18. Processional chants accompany an action. In some cases they have another function. … Not only does [the communion processional song] accompany movement, and thus give order to the assembly, it also assists each communicant in the realization and achievement of "the joy of all" and the fellowship of those "who join their voices in a single song." (GIRM 56i [86])

Reflection

The Communion chant expresses the spiritual union of the communicants by means of the unity of their voices "to show of joy of heart, and to highlight more clearly the 'communitarian' nature of the procession to receive communion" (GIRM no. 86). Its simple character should foster participation by all. The Communion Rite, as all liturgy, is something the members of the congregation do together.

Suggested Questions for Discussion

1. What is the purpose of the Communion chant?
2. What type of texts are appropriate?
3. What type of singing is appropriate? Psalmody? Hymnody?
4. By whom is the Communion chant to be sung?
5. Does the congregation enjoy singing it?
6. When does the singing begin? Why?
7. Is it appropriate to have more than one communion song?
8. Is soft instrumental music ever appropriate? Silence?
9. What is the purpose of reciting the antiphon in the Missal when there is no Communion chant?
10. When do the choir members receive Communion?

51
Purification of the Vessels

Historical Survey

The oldest form of purification after Communion is that known as the ablution of the mouth. This is first attested in the late fourth century when St. John Chrysostom (345–407) advocated that his priests take a little water or eat a piece of bread so that nothing of the sacred species remain in the mouth after Communion. Ordinary wine was used for this purpose in certain monasteries of the west and to some extent was encouraged elsewhere for both priests and laity. This custom lasted, at least in certain areas, till the late Middle Ages. Traces of this particular type of ablution even survived in Masses for the ordination of a priest and for the solemn consecration of a virgin.

From the seventh century onward there gradually appeared the custom of washing the chalice, originally done after the Liturgy, and the purification of the priest's fingers. These were eventually linked to the ablution of the mouth and became normative. The actions were at first done in silence, but soon a number of prayers were added to stimulate the devotion of the priest. It was only with the Missal of Pius V (1570) that these rites and two accompanying prayers became obligatory.

The Order of Mass has simplified this action. If a deacon or instituted acolyte is present, he takes the vessels to the side table where they may be purified immediately or after Mass. In the United States, by virtue of an indult that remains in effect until March 22, 2005, the diocesan Bishop may grant permission for extraordinary ministers to perform this task. The Bishops' Conference requested that this indult be renewed in March 2005.

Documentation

General Instruction of the Roman Missal, Third Typical Edition

163. When the distribution of Communion is finished, the priest himself immediately and completely consumes at the altar any consecrated wine that happens to remain; as for any consecrated hosts that are left, he either consumes them at the altar or carries them to the place designated for the reservation of the Eucharist.
Upon returning to the altar, the priest collects any fragments that may remain. Then, standing at the altar or at the credence table, he purifies the paten or ciborium over the chalice then purifies the chalice, saying quietly, *Quod ore sumpsimus (Lord, may I receive)*, and dries the chalice with a purificator. If the vessels are purified at the altar, they are carried to the credence table by a minister. Nevertheless, it is also permitted, especially if there are several vessels to be purified, to leave them suitably covered on a corporal, either at the altar or at the credence table, and to purify them immediately after Mass following the dismissal of the people.

279. The sacred vessels are purified by the priest, the deacon, or an instituted acolyte

after Communion or after Mass, insofar as possible at the credence table. The purification of the chalice is done with water alone or with wine and water, which is then drunk by whoever does the purification. The paten is usually wiped clean with the purificator.

Care must be taken that whatever may remain of the Blood of Christ after the distribution of Communion is consumed immediately and completely at the altar.

284. When Communion is distributed under both kinds …
   b) Whatever may remain of the Blood of Christ is consumed at the altar by the priest or the deacon or the duly instituted acolyte who ministered the chalice. The same then purifies, wipes, and arranges the sacred vessels in the usual way.

Norms for the Distribution and Reception of Holy Communion Under Both Kinds …

51. After Communion the consecrated bread that remains is to be reserved in the tabernacle. Care should be taken with any fragments remaining on the corporal or in the sacred vessels. The deacon returns to the altar with the priest and collects and consumes any remaining fragments.

52. When more of the Precious Blood remains than was necessary for Communion, and if not consumed by the bishop or priest celebrant, "the deacon immediately and reverently consumes at the altar all of the Blood of Christ which remains; he may be assisted, if needs dictate, by other deacons and priests." (GIRM 182) When there are extraordinary ministers of Communion, they may consume what remains of the Precious Blood from their chalice of distribution with permission of the diocesan bishop.

53. The chalice and other vessels may be taken to a side table, where they are cleansed and arranged in the usual way. Other sacred vessels that held the Precious Blood are purified in the same way as chalices. Provided the remaining consecrated bread has been consumed or reserved and the remaining Precious Blood has been consumed, "it is permissible to leave the vessels … suitably covered and at a side table on a corporal, to be cleansed immediately after Mass following the dismissal of the people." (GIRM 183)

54. The Precious Blood may not be reserved, except for giving Communion to someone who is sick. Only sick people who are unable to receive Communion under the form of bread may receive it under the form of wine alone at the discretion of the priest. If not consecrated at a Mass in the presence of the sick person, the Blood of the Lord is kept in a properly covered vessel and is placed in the tabernacle after Communion. The Precious Blood should be carried to the sick in a vessel that is closed in such a way as to eliminate all danger of spilling. If some of the Precious Blood remains after the sick person has received Communion, it should be consumed by the minister, who should also see to it that the vessel is properly purified.

55. The reverence due to the Precious Blood of the Lord demands that it be fully consumed after Communion is completed and never be poured into the ground or the sacrarium.

Decree. Congregation for Divine Worship and the Discipline of the Sacraments, March 22, 2002

… in virtue of the faculties granted to this Congregation by the Supreme Pontiff, JOHN PAUL II, we grant that in the dioceses of this same Conference [i.e., the Conference of Bishops of the United States of America], for grave pastoral reasons, the faculty may be given by the diocesan Bishop to the priest celebrant to use the assistance, when necessary, even of extraordinary ministers in the cleansing of sacred vessels after the distribution of Communion has been completed in the celebration of Mass. This faculty is conceded for a period of three years as a dispensation from the norm of the *Institutio Generalis, editio typica tertia* of the *Roman Missal*.

Reflection

The purification of the vessels is a functional task. Although performed with reverence, the action should be brief and inconspicuous. It is preferably done after the celebration.

Suggested Questions for Discussion

1. What is the purpose of cleansing the vessels?
2. When and by whom is the accompanying prayer said?
3. Who may wash the vessels? Where?
4. When is it appropriate to purify the vessels at the altar?
5. Are the fingers of the minister to be washed?

52
Silent Prayer/Song Of Praise

Historical Survey

Private prayer after Communion has long been a recommended practice. St. Alphonsus Liguori urged at least a half hour of prayer after the reception of the Eucharist. Pope Pius XII in his Encyclical on the Sacred Liturgy strongly recommended that "priest and faithful ... converse with the Divine Redeemer for at least a short while after Holy Communion." Canon Law warned priests not to forget to make a proper thanksgiving after Mass, and the Roman Missal contains various prayers to nourish his devotion. But most of the faithful, for one reason or another, exited immediately after the celebration. Only a few remained for private prayer.

The Order of Mass now provides times for silent prayer immediately after the distribution of the Eucharist. When this period is of sufficient length to nourish true prayer, the Prayer after Communion serves to sum up the unspoken sentiments of all. As an alternative to silent prayer, however, a hymn of praise may be sung (historically, there are a few isolated instances of such a song after the Communion chant).

Documentation

General Instruction of the Roman Missal, Third Typical Edition

88. When the distribution of Communion is finished, as circumstances suggest, the priest and faithful spend some time praying privately. If desired, a psalm or other canticle of praise or a hymn may also be sung by the entire congregation.

164. Afterwards, the priest may return to the chair. A sacred silence may now be observed for some period of time, or a Psalm or another canticle of praise or a hymn may be sung ...

43. ... and, as circumstances allow, they [the faithful] may sit or kneel while the period of sacred silence after Communion is observed.

45. Sacred silence also, as part of the celebration, is to be observed at the designated times. Its purpose, however, depends on the time it occurs in each part of the celebration. Thus ... after Communion, they [the people] praise and pray to God in their hearts.

Music in Catholic Worship

72. The singing of a psalm or hymn of praise after the distribution of communion is optional. If the organ is played or the choir sings during the distribution of communion, a congregational song may well provide a fitting expression of oneness in the Eucharistic Lord. Since no particular text is specified, there is ample room for creativity.

Reflection

Although a hymn of praise or a psalm may be sung by the entire congregation after the Communion, adequate time for deep and silent prayer should not be rare. Such silence is important to the total rhythm of the celebration.

Suggested Questions for Discussion

1. What is the purpose of the period of silent prayer after Communion?
2. What should be its length?
3. What does it contribute to the rhythm of the Communion Rite?
4. What is the purpose of the song of praise?
5. What texts are appropriate?
6. How does this song differ from the Communion chant?
7. By whom is it sung?
8. May it be replaced by a "meditation" song?
9. On what occasions might a song of praise replace the period of silent prayer?

53
Prayer after Communion

Historical Survey

The desire to express verbally the effects of the Eucharist gave rise to a presidential prayer after the Communion. First appearing in the fifth century and arranged in the manner of the Collect at the beginning of Mass, it was called the "prayer at the conclusion" since it ended the eucharistic celebration. It was also known as the Prayer after Communion or the Postcommunion. Just as the number of opening Collects multiplied during the Middle Ages, so a corresponding series of Postcommunion commemorations was prayed at most celebrations.

Today only one prayer, known as the Prayer after Communion, serves to conclude the Communion Rite. It is preceded by a period of silence, either immediately after the Communion or after the invitation "Let us pray."

Documentation

General Instruction of the Roman Missal, Third Typical Edition

89. To bring to completion the prayer of the People of God, and also to conclude the entire Communion Rite, the priest says the Prayer after Communion, in which he prays for the fruits of the mystery just celebrated.
    In the Mass only one prayer after Communion is said, which ends with a shorter conclusion; that is,
    - If the prayer is directed to the Father: *Per Christum Dominum nostrum*;
    - If it is directed to the Father, but the Son is mentioned at the end: *Qui vivit et regnat in saecula saeculorum*;
    - If it is directed to the Son: *Qui vivis et regnas in saecula saeculorum*.

    The people make the prayer their own by the acclamation, *Amen*.

165. Then, standing at the chair or at the altar and facing the people the priest, with hands joined says, *Oremus (Let us pray)*; then, with hands extended, he recites the prayer after Communion. A brief period of silence may precede the prayer, unless this has been already observed immediately after Communion. At the end of the prayer the people say the acclamation, *Amen*.

Reflection

The prayer after the Communion is not a prayer of thanksgiving; this is rather the nature of the Eucharistic Prayer, particularly in its Preface. It is a prayer asking for the spiritual effects or fruits of the Eucharist.

Suggested Questions for Discussion
1. What is the purpose of the Prayer after Communion?
2. Is any verbal direction needed to indicate that the assembly is to stand for this prayer?
3. Is the prayer preceded by silence?
4. Is it more appropriately prayed at the altar or at the presidential chair?

Concluding Rite

54
General Overview

Historical Survey

Although the early celebration of the Eucharist seems to have ended immediately with its distribution, Christians soon felt a psychological need to round off the Liturgy with a concluding rite. Most frequently this was done by a simple dismissal which was often preceded by a blessing of the people. In both east and west this simple conclusion tended to expand. The Roman Missal of 1570, for example, called for a veneration of the altar, a greeting, a dismissal, a prayer preliminary to the blessing, another veneration of the altar, the blessing itself, and a reading of the prologue of the Gospel according to St. John. In 1884 Pope Leo XIII prescribed that certain prayers be said after Mass.

The Order of Mass has greatly simplified and given a better structure to the concluding rites. Should there be any necessary announcements, these are made first. Then the priest greets and blesses the people. The dismissal is given, and the priest reverences the altar by a kiss before he and the other ministers depart.

When another liturgical rite is added at the end of Mass, the customary concluding rites are omitted.

Documentation

General Instruction of the Roman Missal, Third Typical Edition

90. The concluding rites consist of:
    a) Brief announcements, if they are necessary;
    b) The priest's greeting and blessing, which on certain days and occasions is enriched and expressed in the prayer over the People or another more solemn formula;
    c) The dismissal of the people by the deacon or the priest, so that each may go out to do good works, praising and blessing God;
    d) The kissing of the altar by the priest and the deacon, followed by a profound bow to the altar by the priest, the deacon, and the other ministers.

170. If, however, another liturgical action follows the Mass, the concluding rites, that is, the greeting, the blessing, and the dismissal, are omitted.

Music in Catholic Worship

49. The concluding rite consists of the priest's greeting and blessing, which is sometimes expanded by the prayer over the people or another solemn form, and the dismissal which sends forth each member of the congregation to do good works, praising and blessing the Lord (GIRM 57 [90]).

    A recessional song is optional. The greeting, blessing, dismissal, and recessional song or instrumental music ideally form one continuous action which may culminate in the priest's personal greetings and conversations at the church door.

Reflection

The concluding rite, whose primary elements are the priest's blessing and the dismissal, exhorts the faithful to derive fruits from the celebration by going forth to serve one another and all who live in the world.

Suggested Questions for Discussion

1. What is the purpose of the concluding rites?
2. What are their major elements?
3. Where does the celebrant stand for the concluding rites?
4. Why are the concluding rites omitted when another liturgical service follows? On what occasions would this occur?

55
Announcements

Historical Survey

The giving of announcements has occurred at various locations within the Roman Mass. In the late seventh-century papal liturgy it was immediately after the Communion of the Pope and before the Communion of the clergy and faithful that the archdeacon announced the time and place of the next papal Mass, probably because non-communicants were accustomed to leave the church at this time. The end of the homily was also considered as an appropriate time to give various notices. Pope Leo the Great (440–461), for example, at the conclusion of his Embertide sermons reminded the faithful of the fast days during the week ahead and invited them to attend the vigil on the eve of the next Sunday. This custom of joining the announcements to the homily was normal till recently.

Announcements are now made immediately following the Prayer after Communion, i.e., in a more logical position as the beginning of the concluding rite.

Documentation

General Instruction of the Roman Missal, Third Typical Edition

166. When the prayer after Communion is concluded, brief announcements to the people may be made, if they are needed.
31. … he [the priest] may also make concluding comments to the entire sacred action before the dismissal.

Reflection

Announcements should be short, necessary, and generally of concern to the whole community. Longer and more particular information is better communicated in other ways, e.g., through the parish bulletin. Since the ambo is reserved for the proclamation of God's word, the announcements are preferably given elsewhere.

Suggested Questions for Discussion

1. What is the purpose of the announcements?
2. Why are they given at this time?
3. May they be given at any other time?
4. Why is it inappropriate to give them immediately before the concluding prayer?
5. By whom should they be given? From where?
6. Is there a tendency to give unnecessary announcements?

56
Greeting and Blessing

Historical Survey

At Rome the earliest form of a concluding blessing seems to have been an oration which immediately followed the Prayer after Communion. The deacon admonished the people to bow before the Lord; the Bishop prayed a formula known as the "Prayer over the People"; and all responded *Amen*. From the time of Pope Gregory (590–604) this blessing was restricted to the season of Lent, perhaps with the intention of making the Prayer over the People a blessing proper to the penitents who were preparing to be reconciled with the Church on Holy Thursday. And yet it still remained a blessing of all the people who, following the example of the penitents, were to spend the forty days in penance and prayer.

An additional and more simple form of blessing gradually began to appear. From at least the late seventh century the Pope silently blessed each section of the congregation as he processed from the altar after the solemn dismissal. Roman practice restricted this blessing to the Bishop alone, but from the eleventh century many parish priests also gave this simple blessing after the dismissal. Formulas appeared in the thirteenth century. This blessing with an accompanying text was included in the Missal of Pius V (1570) and, like that of the Pope, was given after the dismissal.

Today the blessing more logically precedes the dismissal. Three forms are given. After the customary greeting the priest may also give a simple blessing in the name of the Father, Son, and Holy Spirit. On given occasions a solemn blessing may be given. In this case the deacon invites the people to bow; the priest gives three invocations each concluded by the people's *Amen*; then the priest concludes with a simple blessing. The Missal also provides various prayers over the people: the deacon gives an invitation; the priest says a prayer over the congregation to which all respond *Amen*; a simple blessing given by the priest follows.

Documentation

General Instruction of the Roman Missal, Third Typical Edition

167. Then the priest, extending his hands, greets the people, saying, *Dominus vobiscum (The Lord be with you)*. They answer, *Et cum spiritu tuo (And also with you)*. The priest, joining his hands again and then immediately placing his left hand on his breast, raises his right hand and adds, *Benedicat vos omnipotens Deus (May Almighty God Bless you)* and, as he makes the Sign of the Cross over the people, continues, *Pater, et Filius, et Spiritus Sanctus (the Father, and the Son, and the Holy Spirit)*. All answer, *Amen*.

    On certain days and occasions this blessing, in accordance with the rubrics, is expanded and expressed by a prayer over the People or another more solemn formula.

A Bishop blesses the people with the appropriate formula, making the Sign of the Cross three times over the people.

Reflection

To bless God means to praise God for his goodness and wonderful gifts. To bless a person is an action requesting that God continue to extend his generosity. In this final blessing the priest prays that the greatest of all benefits may be given in abundant measure to those who have shared in God's word and Christ's Body. Such an action upon departure is found in the New Testament when Christ, before being taken up into heaven, "raised his hands, and blessed them [the apostles]" (Luke 24:50).

Suggested Questions for Discussion

1. What is the purpose of the greeting?
2. When is it appropriately sung? Recited?
3. What is the purpose of the invitation *Bow your heads* … ? How do people respond to this invitation?
4. How often are the various forms of blessing used?
5. In what sense does the priest give the blessing?
6. How can the triple *Amen* of the assembly in the solemn blessing be encouraged?
7. What solemnity is given to the gesture of blessing?

57 Dismissal

Historical Survey

A formal dismissal of the people by the deacon is found in almost all traditional liturgies. At Rome the customary formula was *Ite missa est*, the Latin *missa* being a technical word for "dismissal," i.e., the breaking up of a meeting, the conclusion of an official assembly. From the fourth century this term was applied to the whole celebration. The Roman formula met with competition from another dismissal which was popular among the Franks, the "Let us bless the Lord." It was this form which gradually replaced the Roman dismissal on less festive occasions or when another service followed the Mass. The response to both formulas was "Thanks be to God." Since the *Ite missa est* was considered an expression of joy, it was eventually replaced in Masses for the dead by the "May they rest in peace."

The Missal gives three dismissal forms. The words *Go in peace*, found in all three, are scriptural (see, e.g., Mark 5:34) and occur in various eastern liturgies. The dismissal is given by the deacon or, in his absence, by the priest.

Documentation

General Instruction of the Roman Missal, Third Typical Edition
168. Immediately after the blessing, with hands joined, the priest adds, *Ite, missa est (The Mass is ended, go in peace)*, and all answer, *Deo gratias (Thanks be to God)*.

Reflection

The dismissal sends each member out to doing good works, while praising and blessing the Lord. Day by day the Liturgy builds up those within the Church into the Lord's holy temple, into a spiritual dwelling for God (cf. Eph 2:21–22)—an enterprise which will continue until Christ's full stature is achieved (cf. Eph 4:13). Pope John Paul II has often spoken of what some call "the liturgy after the Liturgy." Evangelization based on the Eucharist entails a commitment to put the Church's social teaching into practice by promoting justice, particularly for our neediest brothers and sisters. The poor, the sick, the elderly who have been neglected, prisoners, those with physical or psychological disabilities, those enslaved by drug addiction, those marginalized because of unemployment, the young without horizons of hope, are numerous forms of the challenging presence of Christ himself who we worship in the Eucharist" (Message to the people of Spain on the first anniversary of the 45th Eucharistic Congress in Seville, 5 June 1994). And also: "The Eucharistic celebration does not stop at the church door" (Apostolic Letter, On Keeping the Lord's Day Holy, *Dies Domini*, no. 45). In a word, the people are now sent forth to carry out the mission of the Church, a mission of healing, justice, and proclamation. All liturgy has a social dimension.

Suggested Questions for Discussion
1. What is the purpose of the dismissal?
2. May its formulas be altered to accord with the occasion? Within what limits?
3. Should the dismissal be sung?
4. In what way has "the Mass ... ended"?

58
Veneration of the Altar

Historical Survey
The kissing of the altar at the conclusion of the Liturgy is a tradition found in many rites. The nature of this farewell gesture was gradually obscured in the Roman Liturgy by a number of developments. The blessing given by the presiding minister as he left the sanctuary was changed into a concluding blessing for all and made an official part of the Mass. The final salutation of the altar, eventually accompanied by a private prayer, preceded this blessing. This kiss was interpreted as a sign of the priest receiving the blessing from Christ before imparting it to the people. The rite was made still more complex by the fact that the priest also kissed the altar before giving the greeting which preceded the dismissal. This action was understood as a sign that the priest's wish for the faithful might also come from Christ represented by the altar.

Today the priest kisses the altar only once at the end of the celebration. The gesture occurs after the dismissal so that its valedictory character is apparent.

Documentation
General Instruction of the Roman Missal, Third Typical Edition
169. Then, as a rule, the priest venerates the altar with a kiss and, after making a profound bow with the lay ministers, departs with them.

Reflection
The kiss of farewell at the end of the celebration mirrors the kiss whereby the altar is greeted at the beginning of Mass. Both are gestures venerating the table as the symbol of Christ. The farewell kiss looks back to the Eucharist which has just concluded and anticipates the next occasion when the community will assemble at the table of the Lord.

Suggested Questions for Discussion
1. What is the purpose of kissing the altar at the end of the celebration?
2. How is the gesture understood by the people?
3. In what manner is it accomplished?
4. Is any other act of veneration made at this time?
5. What is the pace of the procession?
6. What happens after the procession?

59
Recessional

Historical Survey

Medieval Mass books often contained various texts to accompany the recession of the priest, e.g., Daniel 3:57–88 and Psalm 150. These never became an integral part of the rite but, as private devotions of the minister, were eventually included in the Missal as prayers for his thanksgiving after Mass. Neither the Roman nor the eastern rites concluded the celebration with song. And yet in order to give the celebration a certain liturgical and musical unity it was often customary for the choir and at times even the assembly to sing as the ministers departed from the sanctuary.

Although the Order of Mass follows tradition and does not require music to accompany the departure of the ministers, in most parishes the people or the choir sing a recessional song.

Documentation

Music in Catholic Worship

73. The recessional song has never been an official part of the rite; hence musicians are free to plan music which provides an appropriate closing to the liturgy. A song is one possible choice. However, if the people have sung a song after communion, it may be advisable to use only an instrumental or choir recessional.

Reflection

The use of a recessional song is one means of prolonging the festive character of the celebration. Ordinarily brief and well-known, it expresses praise or reflects the particular day or season. Instrumental music may also serve to provide a joyful concluding atmosphere. Silence, especially on occasions of a penitential nature, may also be appropriate.

Suggested Questions for Discussion

1. What is the purpose of a recessional?
2. What forms may it take?
3. What factors influence the choice of a particular form?
4. Should the ministers remain in the sanctuary during the recessional?

Selected Bibliography

The following selection of books, articles, and documents is divided into three sections for the purpose of studying the Order of Mass.

Part I, *Documentation*, lists the basic documents of the Holy See promulgating the reform of the eucharistic liturgy and selected documentation of the Bishops' Committee on the Liturgy of the National Conference of Bishops on various aspects of eucharistic reform.

Part II, *History and Theology*, includes some of the more important studies on the Eucharist, as well as books collecting ancient liturgical sources.

Part III, *The New Order of Mass*, contains books and articles on the Order of Mass in the Missal of Paul VI as well as studies on particular structural elements of this ordo.

I. Documentation

Second Vatican Council. Constitution on the Sacred Liturgy, December 4, 1963 ("Sacrosanctum Concilium"). Washington D.C.: USCC Publications Office, 1964.

Bishops' Committee on the Liturgy. *General Intercessions*. Washington, D.C.: USCC Publications Office, 1979.

Bishops' Committee on the Liturgy. *Liturgical Music Today*. Washington, D.C.: USCC Publications Office, 1982.

Bishops' Committee on the Liturgy. *Music in Catholic Worship*. Revised Edition. Washington, D.C.: USCC Publications Office, 1983.

Bishops' Committee on the Liturgy. *The Body of Christ*. Washington, D.C.: USCC Publications Office, 1977.

Bishops' Committee on the Liturgy. *The Sign of Peace*. Washington, D.C.: USCC Publications Office, 1977.

Hoffman, Elizabeth, ed. *The Liturgy Documents: A Parish Resource*. Third Edition. Chicago: Liturgy Training Publications, 1991.

International Commission on English in the Liturgy. *Documents on the Liturgy 1963–1979: Conciliar, Papal, and Curial Texts*. Collegeville: The Liturgical Press, 1982.

II. History and Theology

Cabié, Robert. *History of the Mass*. Tr. Lawrence J. Johnson. Washington, D.C.: The Pastoral Press, 1992.

Cabié, Robert. *The Eucharist*. Vol. 2 of *The Church at Prayer*. Ed. A.G. Martimort. Tr. Matthew J. O'Connell. Collegeville: The Liturgical Press, 1986.

Crichton, J. D. *Christian Celebration: The Mass*. London: G. Chapman, 1971.

Deiss, Lucien. *Springtime of the Liturgy: Liturgical Texts of the First Four Centuries.* Tr. Matthew J. O'Connell. Collegeville: The Liturgical Press, 1979.

Deiss, Lucien. *The Mass.* Collegeville: The Liturgical Press, 1992.

Dix, Gregory. *The Shape of the Liturgy.* Westminster: Dacre Press, 1945. With Additional Note by Paul V. Marshall. New York: Seabury Press, 1983.

Emminghaus, Johannes H. *The Eucharist: Essence, Form, Celebration.* Tr. Matthew J. O'Connell. Collegeville: The Liturgical Press, 1978.

Foley, Edward. *From Age to Age: How Christians Celebrated the Eucharist.* Chicago: Liturgy Training Publications, 1991.

Jungmann, Joseph A. *The Mass of the Roman Rite: Its Origins and Development (Missarum Sollemnia).* Tr. F. Brunner. 2 Vols. New York: Benziger, 1951–1955.

Jungmann, Joseph A. *The Mass of the Roman Rite: Its Origins and Development (Missarum Sollemnia).* Tr. F. Brunner. Rev. Charles K. Riepe. New York: Benziger Brothers, 1959.

Marrevee, William. *The Popular Guide to the Mass.* Washington, D.C.: The Pastoral Press, 1992.

Sheppard, Lancelot, ed. *The New Liturgy: A Comprehensive Introduction.* London: Darton, Longman and Todd, Ltd. 1970.

White, Susan J. "Eucharist, History of, in the West." In *The New Dictionary of Sacramental Worship.* Ed. Peter E. Fink. Collegeville: The Liturgical Press, 1990. 417–422.

III. The New Order of Mass

General Works

Coughlan, Peter. "The New Order of Mass." *The Furrow* 20 (June 1969) 67–72.

Johnson, Lawrence J. *The Word & Eucharist Handbook.* San Jose, CA: Resource Publications, 1986.

McGoldrick, Patrick. "Aspects of the Order of Mass." *The Furrow* 20 (December 1969) 657–664.

McManus, Frederick R. "The Genius of the Roman Rite Revisited." *Worship* 54 (July 1980) 360–378.

Roguet, A.M. *The New Mass.* Tr. Walter van de Putte. New York: Catholic Book Publishing Co., 1970.

Ryan, Vincent. "The New Mass Rite." *Doctrine and Life* 20 (January 1970) 3–12; (February 1970) 91–101.

Ryder, A. "The Theology of the New Order of Mass." *The Clergy Review* 55 (February 1970) 101–111.

Introductory Rites

Hannon, Kenneth. "Gathering Rites." In *The New Dictionary of Sacramental Worship*. Ed. Peter E. Fink. Collegeville: The Liturgical Press, 1990. 491–494.

Keifer, Ralph A. "And So to Begin: The Introductory Rite." In *To Give Thanks and Praise*. Washington, D.C.: The National Association of Pastoral Musicians, 1980. 105–115.

Keifer, Ralph A. "Our Cluttered Vestibule: The Unreformed Entrance Rite." *Worship* 48:5 (May 1974) 270–277.

Searle, Mark. "Semper Reformanda: The Opening and Closing Rites of the Mass." In *Shaping English Liturgy*. Ed. Peter C. Finn and James M. Schellman. Washington, D.C.: The Pastoral Press, 1990. 53–92.

Liturgy of the Word

Ciferni, Andrew D. "Word, Liturgy of the." In *The New Dictionary of Sacramental Worship*. Ed. Peter E. Fink. Collegeville: The Liturgical Press, 1990. 1320–1323.

Cobb, Peter G. "The Eucharist: The Liturgy of the Word in the Early Church." In *The Study of Liturgy*. Ed. C. Jones and others. New York: Oxford University Press, 1978. 179–188.

Jungmann, Joseph A. *Liturgy of the Word*. London: Burns & Oates, 1966.

Keifer, Ralph A. *To Hear and Proclaim*. Washington, D.C.: The Pastoral Press, 1983.

Keifer, Ralph A. "Wordy Liturgy or Liturgy of the Word." In *To Give Thanks and Praise*. Washington, D.C.: The Pastoral Press, 1980. 117–125.

Milner, Paulinus. "The Purpose and Structure of the Liturgy of the Word." In *The Ministry of the Word*. Ed. Paulinus Milner. London: Burns & Oates, 1967. 11–26.

Liturgy of the Eucharist: Early History

Delorme, J., ed. *The Eucharist in the New Testament*. Baltimore: Helicon, 1964.

Kilmartin, E. *The Eucharist in the Primitive Church*. Englewood Cliffs, NJ: Prentice-Hall, 1965.

Kodell, Jerome. *The Eucharist in the New Testament*. Wilmington, DE: Michael Glazier, 1988.

Liturgy of the Eucharist: Preparation of the Gifts

Keifer, Ralph A. "Preparation of the Altar and the Gifts or Offertory." *Worship* 48:10 (December 1974) 595–600.

Keifer, Ralph A. "The Offertory: The Church's Real Offering." In *To Give Thanks and Praise*. Washington, D.C.: The National Association of Pastoral Musicians, 1980. 133–138.

LeBlanc, Paul J. "Preparation of Altar and Gifts: A Review." *Liturgy* 21:10 (December 1976) 308–311.

McManus, Frederick R. "The Roman Order of Mass from 1964–1969: The Preparation of the Gifts." In *Shaping the English Liturgy*. Ed. Peter C. Finn and James M. Schellman. Washington, D.C.: The Pastoral Press, 1990. 107–138.

Liturgy of the Eucharist: The Eucharistic Prayer

"The Eucharistic Prayer." *Pastoral Music* 10:2 (December–January 1986). Complete issue.

Bouyer, Louis. *Eucharist: Theology and Spirituality of the Eucharistic Prayer*. Notre Dame: University of Notre Dame Press, 1968.

Dallen, James. "Spirituality of the Eucharistic Prayer." *Worship* 58:4 (July 1984) 359–372.

Kavanagh, Aidan. "Thoughts on the Roman Anaphora." *Worship* 39 (November 1965) 515–529.

Keifer, Ralph A. "The Eucharistic Prayer." In *To Give Thanks and Praise*. Washington, D.C.: The National Association of Pastoral Musicians, 1980. 139–151.

Ligier, Louis. "From the Last Supper to the Eucharist." In *The New Liturgy*. Ed. Lancelot Sheppard. London: Darton, Longman & Todd, 1970. 113–150.

Moloney, Raymond. *Our Eucharistic Prayers in Worship, Preaching & Study*. Theology and Life Series, Vol. 14. Wilmington, DE: Michael Glazier, 1985.

Ryan, John Barry. "Eucharistic Prayers." In *The New Dictionary of Sacramental Worship*. Ed. Peter E. Fink. Collegeville: The Liturgical Press, 1990. 451–459.

Smolarski, Dennis C. *Eucharistia: A Study of the Eucharistic Prayer*. Ramsey, NJ: The Paulist Press, 1982.

Soubigou, Louis. *A Commentary on the Prefaces and the Eucharistic Prayers of the Roman Missal*. Tr. John A. Otto. Collegeville: the Liturgical Press, 1971.

Liturgy of the Eucharist: The Communion Rite

Ciferni, Andrew. "The Communion Rite." *Assembly* 14:4 (June 1988) 406–407.

Gallagher, Patricia A. "The Communion Rite." *Worship* 63:4 (July 1989) 316–327.

Huck, Gabe. *The Communion Rite at Sunday Mass*. Chicago: Liturgy Training Publications, 1989.

Keifer, Ralph A. "When We Eat This Bread … : The Communion Rite." In *To Give Thanks and Praise*. Washington, D.C.: The National Association of Pastoral Musicians, 1980. 153–157.

Taft, Robert. "Receiving Communion: A Forgotten Symbol?" *Worship* 57:5 (September 1983) 412–418.

Concluding Rite

Searle, Mark. "Semper Reformanda: The Opening and Closing Rites of the Mass." In *Shaping English Liturgy*. Ed. Peter C. Finn and James M. Schellman. Washington, D.C.: The Pastoral Press, 1990. 53–92.